Nurturing Character in the Classroom
Ethical Sensitivity
EthEx Series Book 1

Nurturing Character in the Classroom, EthEx Series

Ethical Sensitivity
Ethical Judgment
Ethical Motivation
Ethical Action

CURRICULUM & COURSE-BASED TEXTS & RESOURCES DIVISION

Alliance for Catholic Education Press
at the University of Notre Dame

Nurturing Character in the Classroom
Ethical Sensitivity
EthEx Series Book 1

Darcia Narvaez, Ph.D.
Leilani Gjellstad Endicott, Ph.D.

ALLIANCE FOR CATHOLIC EDUCATION PRESS
AT THE UNIVERSITY OF NOTRE DAME

Notre Dame, Indiana

Alliance for Catholic Education Press
at the University of Notre Dame
158 IEI Building
Notre Dame, IN 46556
http://www.nd.edu/~acepress

Text design by Tonia Bock
Cover design by Mary Jo Adams Kocovski

ISBN: 978-0-9819501-0-5

Library of Congress Cataloging-in-Publication Data

Narvaez, Darcia.
  Ethical sensitivity / Darcia Narvaez, Leilani Gjellstad Endicott.
     p. cm. -- (Nurturing character in the classroom, EthEx series ; bk. 1)
  Includes bibliographical references.
  Summary: "Provides a framework and instructional materials for integrating ethical education, specifically
ethical sensitivity, into the middle school classroom and curriculum"--Provided by publisher.
  ISBN 978-0-9819501-0-5 (pbk. : alk. paper)
  1. Moral education (Middle school)--United States 2. Ethics--Study and teaching (Middle school)--United
States   I. Endicott, Leilani Gjellstad, 1975- II. Title.

  LC268.N239 2009
  370.11'4--dc22
                                     2009004033

This book was printed on acid-free paper.

Printed in the United States of America.

Table of Contents

Foreword

For the past several years my colleagues and I at the University of Minnesota, in partnership with the Minnesota Department of Children, Families and Learning, have been developing a model for character education in the middle grades that we call "Community Voices and Character Education." Here are the six key characteristics of our model.

First, we adopt a <u>skills-based understanding</u> of moral character. This is not a new idea. Plato believed that the just person is like an artisan who has particular, highly-cultivated skills that have been developed through training and practice (Plato, 1987). Persons of good character, then, have better developed skills in four areas: ethical sensitivity, ethical judgment, ethical motivation, and ethical action (Narvaez, Mitchell, Endicott, & Bock, 1999). For example, experts in the skills of Ethical Sensitivity are better at quickly and accurately "reading" a moral situation and determining what role they might play (Narvaez & Endicott, 2009). Experts in the skills of Ethical Judgment have many tools for solving complex moral problems (Narvaez & Bock, 2009). Experts in the skills of Ethical Motivation cultivate an ethical identity that leads them to prioritize ethical goals (Narvaez & Lies, 2009). Experts in the skills of Ethical Action know how to keep their "eye on the prize," enabling them to stay on task and take the necessary steps to get the ethical job done (Narvaez, 2009). Our approach to character development, then, insists on a holistic understanding of the moral person (Narvaez, Bock, & Endicott, 2003). It views character as a set of component skills that can be cultivated to high levels of expertise.

Expertise is a notion that has gained prominence among educational researchers (e.g., Sternberg, 1998, 1999). According to this view, children move along a continuum from novice-to-expert in each content domain that they study. Unlike novices, experts have larger, more complex and better organized knowledge (Chi, Glaser, & Farr, 1988; Sternberg, 1998). Experts see the world differently (Neisser, 1967). Their extensive pattern matching capabilities allow experts to notice things that novices miss (Novick, 1988). Experts possess well-developed sets of procedural skills. Unlike novices, experts know *what* knowledge to access, *which* procedures to apply, *how* to apply them, and *when* it is appropriate (Abernathy & Hamm, 1995; Hogarth, 2001).

Second, to help children develop character skills in the way that experts do, we adopt a <u>scientifically-based</u>, cognitive approach to <u>learning and teaching</u> that assumes that children actively construct representations of the world (Narvaez, 2002; Piaget, 1932/1965, 1952, 1970). <u>Best practice instruction</u> provides opportunities for students to develop more accurate and better organized representations and the procedural skills required to use them (Anderson, 1989). Like the expert, students learn to master the defining features and underlying structures of a domain through practice that is focused, extensive, and coached (Ericsson & Charness, 1994; Ericsson, Krampe, & Tesch-Roemer, 1993). The educator provides authentic learning experiences that are structured according to what we know about levels of apprenticeship (Marshall, 1995; Rogoff, Baker-Sennett, Lacasa, & Goldsmith, 1995).

Third, our model insists that character development be <u>embedded within standards-driven academic instruction</u>, for ultimately this is the only way character education will be sustained.

Fourth, character should be <u>taught across the curriculum in every subject and activity</u>, for character skills are required not in isolation but throughout every encounter in life.

Fifth, our model opens character education to <u>greater accountability</u>, in the sense that skills are teachable and progress toward mastery can be measured.

Sixth, a curricular approach to character education must be an <u>intentional collaboration</u> with "community voices." After all, students are apprentices <u>to the community</u>. The issue of "whose values will be taught?" is best approached by embedding educational goals within the value commitments of particular communities.

Does this model work? Our preliminary data are quite promising. For example, classrooms using our approach showed increases in scores on prosocial responsibility, ethical identity, and prosocial risk-taking, while a comparison group did not.

In summary, moral character is best thought of as a set of teachable, ethically-relevant skills. Ethical skill instruction should be embedded in standards-driven pedagogy. Ethical skills should be taught across the curriculum and cultivated by community voices. With such an education, students will develop schemas of goodness and of justice. They will learn routines of helping and of reasoning. They will learn skills of leadership and of commitment. With these skills they can take responsibility for ethical action in their neighborhoods and in their communities. They will be energized by memories of personal ethical action. With these skills, students are empowered to be active citizens who will make the fate of the nation their own.

Speech at the Whitehouse Conference on Character and Community
Darcia Narvaez, Ph.D.
Associate Professor, University of Notre Dame
June 2002

References

Abernathy, C. M., & Hamm, R. M. (1995). *Surgical intuition*. Philadelphia: Hanley & Belfus.

Anderson, L. M. (1989). Learners and learning. In M. C. Reynolds (Ed.), *Knowledge base for the beginning teacher* (pp. 85-99). Oxford: Pergamon Press.

Chi, M. T. H., Glaser, R., & Farr, M. (1988*). The nature of expertise*. Hillsdale, NJ: Erlbaum.

Ericsson, K. A., & Charness, N. (1994). Expert performance: Its structure and acquisition. *American Psychologist, 49,* 725-747.

Ericsson, K. A., Krampe, R. T., & Tesch-Roemer, C. (1993). The role of deliberate practice in the acquisition of expert performance. *Psychological Review, 100*(3), 363-406.

Hogarth, R. M. (2001). *Educating intuition*. Chicago: University of Chicago Press.

Marshall, S. P. (1995). *Schemas in problem solving*. Cambridge: Cambridge University Press.

Narvaez, D. (2002). Does reading moral stories build character? *Educational Psychology Review, 14*(2), 155-171.

Narvaez, D. (2009). *Ethical action: Nurturing character in the classroom, EthEx Series, Book 4*. Notre Dame, IN: Alliance for Catholic Education Press.

Narvaez, D., & Bock, T. (2009). *Ethical judgment: Nurturing character in the classroom, EthEx Series, Book 2*. Notre Dame, IN: Alliance for Catholic Education Press.

Narvaez, D., Bock, T., & Endicott, L. (2003). Who should I become? Citizenship, goodness, moral flourishing, and ethical expertise. In W. Veugelers & F. Oser (Eds.), *Teaching in moral and democratic education*. Bern: P. Lang.

Narvaez, D., & Endicott, L. (2009*). Ethical sensitivity: Nurturing character in the classroom, EthEx Series, Book 1*. Notre Dame, IN: Alliance for Catholic Education Press.

Narvaez, D., & Lies, J. (2009). *Ethical motivation: Nurturing character in the classroom, EthEx Series, Book 3*. Notre Dame, IN: Alliance for Catholic Education Press.

Narvaez, D., Mitchell, C., Endicott, L., & Bock, T. (1999). *Nurturing character in the middle school classroom: A guidebook for teachers*. St. Paul, MN: Department of Children, Families, and Learning.

Neisser, U. (1967). *Cognitive psychology*. New York: Appletown-Century-Crofts.

Novick, L. R. (1988). Analogical transfer, problem similarity, and expertise. *Journal of Experimental Psychology: Learning, Memory, & Cognition, 14*(3), 510-520.

Piaget, J. (1952). *The origin of intelligence in children*. New York: International University Press.

Piaget, J. (1965*). The moral judgment of the child* (M. Gabain, Trans.). New York: Free Press. (Original work published 1932)

Piaget, J. (1970). *Genetic epistemology* (E. Duckworth, Trans.). New York: Columbia University Press.

Plato. (1987). *The republic*. London: Penguin.

Rogoff, B., Baker-Sennett, J., Lacasa, P., & Goldsmith, D. (1995). Development through participation in sociocultural activity. *Cultural Practices as Contexts for Development: New Directions for Child and Adolescent Development, 67,* 45-64.

Sternberg, R. (1998). Abilities are forms of developing expertise. *Educational Researcher, 3,* 22-35.

Sternberg, R. (1999). Intelligence as developing expertise. *Contemporary Educational Psychology, 24*(4), 359-375.

Preface

The *Nurturing Character in the Classroom, EthEx Series* materials were developed under the auspices of the Minnesota Community Voices and Character Education project (grant# R215V980001 from the U. S. Department of Education Office of Educational Research and Improvement to the Minnesota Department of Children, Families and Learning during 1998-2002).

The *Nurturing Character in the Classroom, EthEx Series* materials were developed in collaboration with teachers across the state of Minnesota and were tested throughout the project by volunteer teams of educators. **For a report of the final-year evaluation, see Narvaez, Bock, Endicott, and Lies (2004).**

EthEx refers to the lifelong development of ethical skills toward expertise (**eth**ical **ex**pertise) in many domains and situations. The four EthEx books (sensitivity, judgment, motivation, action) suggest skills and subskills required for virtuous life. The books also lay out how to teach them through four levels of expertise development.

EthEx is incorporated into the **Integrative Ethical Education** model (Narvaez, 2006, 2007, 2008, in press). The Integrative Ethical Education model has five steps for educators including (along with EthEx) the importance of a caring relationship with each student, a supportive climate (for achievement and character), student self-regulation for character and achievement, and restoring community networks and support.

These booklets were developed for the middle school level (ages 11-15), but elementary and high school teachers have used them successfully as well.

For **staff development** in your school, please contact Darcia Narvaez at the University of Notre Dame, Department of Psychology (dnarvaez@nd.edu). For questions or other materials, also contact Dr. Narvaez.

References

Narvaez, D. (2006). Integrative ethical education. In M. Killen & J. Smetana (Eds.), *Handbook of moral development* (pp. 703-733). Mahwah, NJ: Erlbaum.

Narvaez, D. (2007). How cognitive and neurobiological sciences inform values education for creatures like us. In D. Aspin & J. Chapman (Eds.), *Values education and lifelong learning: Philosophy, policy, practices* (pp. 127-159). Dordrecht, The Netherlands: Springer Press International.

Narvaez, D. (2008). Human flourishing and moral development: Cognitive science and neurobiological perspectives on virtue development. In L. Nucci & D. Narvaez (Eds.), *Handbook of moral and character education* (pp. 310-327). New York: Routledge.

Narvaez, D. (in press). *Moral development: A pragmatic approach to fostering engagement and imagination.*

Narvaez, D., Bock, T., Endicott, L., & Lies, J. (2004). Minnesota's voices and character education project. *Journal of Research in Character Education, 2,* 89-112.

Acknowledgments

Thanks to former University of Minnesota Team Members and affiliates whose ideas or efforts were influential at one point or another in the development of materials: Christyan Mitchell, Jolynn Gardner, Ruth Schiller, and Laura Staples.

Thanks to Connie Anderson, Minnesota Department of Children, Families and Learning, for her wisdom and leadership throughout the Community Voices and Character Education Project.

Special thanks to our school-based collaborators from across the state of Minnesota who kept us focused on what really works and what really helps the classroom teacher.

Introduction
to the
Ethical Expertise Model
(EthEx)

Purpose and Goals of the EthEx Model

At the beginning of the 21st century, children are less likely to spend time under adult supervision than they were in the past. As a result, children's ethical education has become haphazard, and subject to strong influence from popular media. To help the development of children, we seek to assist educators develop curricula that teach character while simultaneously meeting regular academic requirements. We apply research-based theory to instruction for ethical development, using an expertise model of ethical behavior that is based on research and applied to ethics education.

The Four Guide Books for Teachers

We have created four books[1] that address the four main psychological processes involved in behaving ethically: Ethical Sensitivity, Ethical Judgment, Ethical Motivation, and Ethical Action. Each book provides suggestions for ways to work on the skills of the process within regular lessons. Each book links ethics education to regular academic requirements. The four books are designed to help teachers develop a conscious and conscientious approach to helping students build character.

Why Not a Curriculum?

There are several problems with set curricula. First, the lessons are written out of the context of the classroom for which they are designed to be used. Consequently, no pre-fabricated lesson is actually taught exactly as designed because the teacher must adapt it to the students and class at hand. Second, we have seen too many curricula used once or twice and set aside as other demands claim teacher attention. So, although a set curriculum may appear more useful to the teacher at the outset, in the end it can become "old" as the latest mandate takes precedence. Third, an outside, packaged curriculum is often not assimilated into the teacher's way of thinking about instruction. Hence, it may feel "alien" to the teacher, a feeling that is correspondingly felt by students. So we believe that the best way to change teaching over the long term is to help teachers modify what they already teach. We make suggestions for changes, but the teacher herself modifies lessons in ways that work for her and her students. We believe that teacher tailoring is an approach that can bring lasting change.

[1] These materials have been developed under the auspices of grant # R215V980001 from the U.S. Department of Education Office of Educational Research and Improvement.

Should Teachers Teach Values?
They already are

To educate a person in mind and not in morals is to educate a menace to society.
-Theodore Roosevelt

The United States at the beginning of the 21st century has reached a new pinnacle. There is more prosperity throughout the society than ever before. There are more equal rights across groups (e.g., males and females, minorities and majorities) than at any time in the history of the world. There are comforts U.S. citizens enjoy that are accessible only to the wealthy in many other nations of the world (e.g., clean water, sewage, inexpensive clothes, and food). Then why are children around the nation shooting their peers at school? Why do so many lament our public behavior and sense of community? Why do some argue that our social supports are the worst among industrialized countries of the world (e.g., no national day care, few national benefits for parents)? Why does the U.S. have a greater percentage of its citizens imprisoned than any other nation save Russia? Certainly there are multiple causes for these outcomes. Many people, however, are concerned about the cultural health of our nation.

What do you think of our nation's cultural health? Take, for example, current standards for public behavior—are they better or worse than in the past? What do you think of popular culture? Television shows use language, discuss topics, and show interactions that would not have been broached just a few years ago. For the sake of entertainment, committed couples allow themselves to be placed on "Temptation Island" in order to test how committed they really are. Is that all right? On the popular show "The Ozbournes" the parents fully use profanity. Does it matter? Professional athletes can be felons and still receive acclaim from fans and the news media. Should we care? Many have noted that citizens are increasingly impatient, self-absorbed, and rude in public. Have you noticed? Most notably, people are harming and killing others over traffic offenses (e.g., Road Rage Summit, Minneapolis, April 29, 1999).

Citizens of other industrialized nations are appalled by our culture and consider us a nation of self-indulgent adolescents:

> Americans are like children: noisy, curious, unable to keep a secret, not given to subtlety, and prone to misbehave in public. Once one accepts the American's basically adolescent nature, the rest of their culture falls into place and what at first seemed thoughtless and silly appears charming and energetic. (Faul, 1994, p. 5)

Do you agree? Do you believe that individuals in the United States overemphasize their rights with little thought for their responsibilities to others? Do they (we) overemphasize individualism at the expense of collective goals as communitarians contend (e.g., Bellah, Madsen, Sullivan, Swidler, & Tipton, 1985; Etzioni, 1994)? According to this perspective, everyone is rushing from one activity to another with little thought for neighbors. The patience that is learned from long-time interaction with neighbors is not being fostered. Instead, impatience with others seems the norm. Miss Manners concurs, believing that we have a civility crisis.

Consider today's families. At the dawn of the 21st century in the United States, it is normal for parents (supported by corresponding laws and social beliefs) to think of themselves as individuals first and family members second, making it easy to divorce a spouse even when there are children. Even as a single parent works hard to support the family (or both parents work to maintain a standard of living formerly supported by one income), many are unable to provide the support and supervision their children need (Steinberg, 1996). As a result, children are not getting enough adult attention. A third of them are depressed. Too many commit suicide. They turn to their peers for values, support, and goals.[2] Children spend more time with television, with all its contemporary crudities, than with their parents. Children's values are cultivated willy-nilly by their daily experience largely apart from adults. Some young people admire Eminem, a White rap singer whose songs are replete with the raping or killing of women (including his mother). In fact, some sociologists and philosophers have suggested that U.S. culture, in its fascination with killing, is a culture not only of violence but of death. Such are the values that children bring to school.

"So what?" you might say. "I try not to make judgments about the cultures of my students. I let the students make up their own minds. I don't teach values in my classroom." Really? Is any behavior acceptable in your room? If not, you are teaching values; you are indicating that some behaviors are better than others. Not hitting is better than hitting. Not cheating is better than cheating. On a daily basis, you decide which students or behaviors get rewarded and which get punished. Teachers make decisions about how "the benefits and burdens of living together are distributed" (Rest, 1986). Teachers decide how to manage the competition and cooperation that humans bring to social interactions. In short, teachers are teaching values all day long.

[2] Unlike most other industrialized nations, there are few social supports outside the home that are built into our system; it was designed to rely on the strength of the nuclear family and extended family. A high rate of single parenting, both parents working and the resultant guilt, lack of parenting skills, lack of extended family support, and a cultural milieu oriented to pleasure rather than self-sacrifice all contribute to the decline in communal satisfaction. Instead of child raising being shared across society, the schools are shouldering the many needs that growing (and neglected or abused) children have.

6

Teachers' Ethical Decisions

We urge teachers to be both conscious of and conscientious about the values they are teaching.

There are many morally-relevant situations in schools in which teachers make decisions that affect student welfare. Here are a few concrete examples of value teaching:

- When teachers **divide the class into groups**, they are conveying what should be noticed (e.g., gender) and what they value (e.g., cooperation, achievement). By doing this they reinforce what students should notice and value.
- When teachers **discipline** students, the students learn what behaviors are important in that classroom (or in the hallway, depending on where the disciplining takes place).
- The **school rules the teacher enforces (or doesn't enforce)** reveal how seriously the students should take rules in school and in general.
- The **standards a teacher applies** to behavior, homework, and attitudes are practiced (and learned) by the students in the classroom.
- **The way a classroom is structured physically** and the way the teacher sets up procedures (and which ones) demonstrate the values held by the teacher. For example, if the teacher wants to emphasize creativity he or she may have colorful decor, alternating seating arrangements, and may allow freedom of choice in selecting academic activities.
- **The teacher's communication style** (quiet and firm, or playful and easy going) can set the climate and convey expectations for behavior.
- Whether or not and how teachers **communicate with parents** show how parents are valued.
- **Grading policies** are another way that teachers distribute the benefits and burdens available in the classroom—does the teacher use norm-references or criterion-references or contract-based grading?
- **Curriculum content selection** can convey a high regard for one culture over another, one viewpoint over another. Whether or not teachers assign homework over religious holidays (and whose holidays) reveal the teacher's expectations and values.
- **The teacher's cultural assumptions** about the social context and his or her instinctive responses to students convey non-verbally who is valued and who is not. This may be one of the most important features of a classroom for a minority student whose success may be at risk.

Intro to the EthEx Model

In short, teachers teach values whether or not they realize it. We urge teachers to be both conscious and conscientious about the values they are teaching. Hence this book has goals for teacher development. As teachers develop curricula using our principles, they will learn the principles to use in their professional behavior. First, we will discuss the process of ethical behavior. Then we will discuss how to apply this knowledge in the classroom—for both curriculum and for general climate in the classroom. Based on these materials, teachers will be able to design activities and a classroom that promote ethical behavior.

This is not to say that teachers currently are without guidance as to promoting an ethical classroom. Teachers have a code of ethics to which they subscribe when obtaining a license and a position. Notice the table from the National Education Association's Code of Ethics. These codes affect much of what teachers decide and do. Notice that the NEA code is not one of "doing no harm," but is proactive, that is, "doing good."

FROM THE CODE OF ETHICS OF THE EDUCATION PROFESSION
(National Education Association, 1975)

Principle 1: Commitment to the student.

In fulfillment to the student, the educator

1. Shall not unreasonably restrain the student from independent action in the pursuit of learning.
2. Shall not unreasonably deny the student access to varying points of view.
3. Shall not deliberately suppress or distort subject matter relevant to the student's progress.
4. Shall make reasonable effort to protect the student from conditions harmful to learning or to health and safety.
5. Shall not intentionally expose the student to embarrassment or disparagement.
6. Shall not on the basis of race, color, creed, sex, national origin, marital status, political or religious beliefs, family, social or cultural background, or sexual orientation, unfairly:
    a. Exclude any student from participation in any program;
    b. Deny benefits to any student;
    c. Grant any advantage to any student.

The NEA code requires teachers:

* to present more than one viewpoint,
* to present the full gamut of subject matter relevant to the student,
* to protect the student from harm.

These are actions that require conscious deliberation. For example, questions the teacher might consider are: What are multiple viewpoints on this topic? What content should be included? What harms students and how can I design an environment and classroom atmosphere that is least harmful? What if a student has a viewpoint that is legitimately harmful or wrong? If the teacher does not deliberately plan around these issues, chances are there will be only mainstream viewpoints presented, the subject matter will be narrow, and the student may have to tolerate insults and other harm from peers.

We believe that there is more to ethical education than even following a code of ethics. The code provides a minimal set of general guidelines. Promoting ethical behavior in students requires not only a deliberate effort but a theory for what ethical behavior entails. In character education programs across the country, it is not always clear what direction these efforts should take. That is the topic of the next section.

What Should Be Taught?
The Process Model of Ethical Behavior

When a curriculum claims to be educating for character, what should it mean? What are the aspects of ethics that should be addressed? As a framework for analysis, we use the process model of ethical behavior as described by Rest (1983) and advocated by Bebeau, Rest, and Narvaez (1999). The model includes ethical sensitivity, ethical judgment, ethical motivation, and ethical action. See the framework outlined below and described in the next section.

The Process Model of Ethical Behavior

 ### ETHICAL SENSITIVITY
NOTICE!
Pick up on the cues related to
ethical decision making and behavior;
Interpret the situation according to who is involved,
what actions to take, and what possible reactions
and outcomes might ensue.

ETHICAL JUDGMENT
THINK!
Reason about the possible actions in the situation
and judge which action is most ethical.

 ### ETHICAL MOTIVATION
AIM!
Prioritize the ethical action over other goals and needs
(either in the particular situation, or as a habit).

ETHICAL ACTION
ACT!
Implement the ethical action by knowing how to do so
and follow through despite hardship

How the Ethical Process Model Works

A kindergarten student in New York City dies midyear from longstanding child abuse at the hands of a parent. The community is shocked that the teacher and school did not prevent the untimely death.

The star of the boy's basketball team is flunking English. If he gets a failing grade, he won't be able to play on the team. Should the teacher give him a passing grade so that the team has a chance to win the championship and boost school morale?

An American Indian student won't look the teacher in the eye nor volunteer answers in class. How should the teacher respond?

From large effects to small, the ethical behavior of teachers—or the lack there-of—influences children's lives on a daily basis (e.g., Bergem, 1990; Goodlad, Soder, & Sirotnik, 1990). Decisions about grading and grouping; decisions about curriculum, instructional style, assessment; decisions about the allotment of time, care, and encouragement (which students, when, where, and how?)—all of these are ethical decisions the educator faces each day. How can teachers sort out the processes of ethical decision making?

First, one must know what ethical behavior looks like. When thinking about ethical behavior, it is often helpful to think of ethical failure. For example, albeit an extreme one, think of the teacher whose student dies from child abuse. How is it that the teacher did not take ethical action and intervene? There are many points at which failure might have occurred. First, the teacher would have to recognize the signs and symptoms of abuse, and have some empathic reaction to the child's circumstance. Having noticed and felt concern, the teacher would need to think about what action might be taken and what outcomes might occur. Then the teacher must reason about the choices and decide which action to take. (In order for ethical behavior to eventually occur, the teacher would need to select an ethical action). Next, the teacher would need to prioritize the chosen (ethical) action over other needs, motives, and goals. Finally, the teacher would need to know what steps to take to implement the decision, and persevere until the action was completed. It is apparent that there are a lot of places where things can go wrong. For example, the teacher may not see the signs or may make a bad judgment or may have other priorities or may not know what to do or may give up in frustration. In effect, ethical failure can stem from any one or more of these weaknesses.

Rest (1983) has asked: What psychological elements are involved in bringing about an ethical action? He has suggested that there are at least four psychological processes of ethical behavior that must occur in order for an ethical behavior to ensue. These four processes are:

(1) *Ethical Sensitivity:* Noticing the cues that indicate a moral situation is at hand. Identifying the persons who are interested in possible actions and outcomes and how the interested parties might respond to the range of possible actions and outcomes.

(2) *Ethical Judgment:* Making a decision about what is ethically right or ethically wrong in the situation.

(3) *Ethical Motivation:* Placing the ethical action choice at the top of one's priorities, over all other personal values at the moment.

(4) *Ethical Action:* Having the necessary ego strength and implementation skills to complete the action despite obstacles, opposition, and fatigue.

In an effort to make these processes clear, let us look at a specific situation in a classroom to which we will apply the processes. Let us imagine that Mr. Anderson has a classroom of children in which Abraham is hitting Maria. Now let us look at each of the processes in relation to this event.

Process 1: Ethical Sensitivity

Picking up on the cues related to ethical decision making and ethical behavior. Interpreting the situation according to who is involved, what actions to take, what possible reactions and outcomes might ensue.

Teachers need to be able to detect and interpret environmental cues correctly in order for the other processes of ethical behavior to be initiated. For example, if Mr. Anderson completely fails to see Abraham hitting Maria, there will be no consideration of action choices or action taken. In order to perceive the action, such an occurrence must be salient because, for example, it is unusual. On the other hand, Mr. Anderson may not notice the hitting if it is a daily class-wide event, or if it is an agreed-upon sign of affection.

Ethical Sensitivity

Notice a problem (sensibilities)
What kinds of problems are salient to me, my family, my community, my affiliative groups?

State the situation (critical thinking)
What is the problem? How did the problem come about? How much time is there to make a decision? How does my community identify the problem? How do elders in my family identify the problem? How does my religion or family culture affect my perceptions?

State the interested parties (critical thinking)
Who are the people who will be affected by this decision (family, community, affiliative groups)? Who should be consulted in this decision? Who has faced this problem before? With whom could I talk about the problem?

Weigh the possible outcomes—short-term and long-term (creative thinking)
What are the possible consequences to me, my family/community/affiliative groups for each possible action? What are the possible reactions of these interested parties? What are the potential benefits for me, my family/community/affinity groups for each possible action? Who else might be affected? How will my choice affect the rest of the world now and in the future?

List all possible options (creative thinking)
How could the problem be solved? What are the choices I have for solving the problem? How would my community/family/cultural group solve the problem? What are the choices my family/cultural/community allow? Should I consider other options?

In intercultural/intersocial-class situations, cue misperception may take place, leading to improper action or no action at all. For example, a middle-class teacher in the U.S.A. may subconsciously perceive the downcast eyes of a Native American student in conversation with her as a sign of disrespect toward her authority. But in the student's own culture, the opposite is the case. However, out of ignorance the teacher may take an action to re-establish her authority, for example, punish the child. In contrast, a child may exhibit disrespectful behavior for his own sub-culture, such as severe slouching for some African-American communities.

However, this action is not really noticed since it is not considered out of the ordinary by the non-African-American teacher or interpreted as a threat to her authority (which it is intended to be) but is considered to be an acceptable expression of frustration on behalf of the student. In this case, the teacher interprets (subconsciously) the child's behavior as a personal freedom issue rather than the challenge to authority (a responsibility issue) that it is.

Ethical sensitivity includes subconscious processing which is often culturally based. As such, teachers need to become aware of their culturally-based expectations and to broaden their understanding of other cultural perspectives in order to circumvent misinterpretation of student behavior.

Not only is Mr. Anderson faced with many perceptual cues to sort through each day, he is also faced with countless situations in which he must make decisions with partial information. Before making a decision, he must interpret situations contextually, according to who is interested in the outcome, what actions and outcomes are possible and how the interested people might react to each. Many problems are much more complicated than in our example (e.g., whether or not to promote a student to the next grade). Here, it is obvious that hitting is generally wrong.

In our incident with Abraham and Maria, Mr. Anderson has noticed the action and finds it out of the ordinary and unacceptable. Now he must determine who is interested in the decision he makes about the incident—certainly Abraham and Maria would be interested, as well as their parents and families, the school administrator, not to speak of the other children in the classroom. Next, he thinks about the actions he could take in this situation and the likely outcomes and reactions of interested parties. For example, he might quickly think:

> Well, I could stop what I am doing and verbally intervene in front of the whole class. Maybe that is not such a good idea because it would disrupt everyone's work. If Abraham does not stop, other children might notice and perhaps think that hitting was permissible. I could walk over there and physically intervene—grab Abraham's hand. That would stop it and still draw attention from the others— maybe they would learn something. Or, I could ignore it, since Abraham tends to do this when he gets excited—he means no harm. But how would Maria react to that? If I don't do something, Maria's parents might complain to the administrator.

Ethical sensitivity involves attending to relevant events and mapping out possible actions and their effects. It includes a subtle interaction between both conscious and subconscious processing.

ETHICAL SENSITIVITY SKILLS

ES-1: Understanding Emotional Expression
ES-2: Taking the Perspective of Others
ES-3: Connecting to Others
ES-4: Responding to Diversity
ES-5: Controlling Social Bias
ES-6: Interpreting Situations
ES-7: Communicating Well

Process 2: Ethical Judgment

*Reasoning about the possible actions in the situation
and judging which action is most ethical.*

Following this exploration of possible actions and reactions, the ethical actor must decide on which course of action to take. Ethical judgment is the process of making a decision about which action of all the options is the most moral action. Lawrence Kohlberg (1984) defined different ways that people make decisions about how to get along with others (see the chart on p. 15). Whereas in ethical sensitivity, cultural differences are particularly important, in moral judgment, normative developmental trends in moral judgment are important. The types of moral reasoning Kohlberg found are developmental and have been identified in dozens of countries around the world. Although there are other types of criteria individuals use to make ethical decisions, Kohlberg's framework has extensive empirical research support. In addition, the vast majority of research shows no gender differences.

Ethical Judgment

Make a decision
What is the best action to take? What choice should I make? Why?

Ethical judgment concerns choosing the ethical action from the choices considered in the process of ethical sensitivity; this decision will be influenced by the ethical reasoning structures of the decision maker. In other words, Mr. Anderson selects the action that is the most ethical in the particular situation according to his level of ethical judgment development. In our scenario, Mr. Anderson may decide that, out of the choices we listed above, going over to Abraham and physically intervening is the most defensible ethical action:

It prevents further harm to Maria, and has ramifications for future behavior by Abraham and the rest of the class. It sends a clear signal both to Abraham and the rest of the class about how the students should NOT treat each other. I can use it as an opportunity to discuss the importance of following rules to keep order and safety in the classroom.

ETHICAL JUDGMENT SKILLS
EJ-1: Reasoning Generally
EJ-2: Reasoning Ethically
EJ-3: Understanding Ethical Problems
EJ-4: Using Codes and Identifying Judgment Criteria
EJ-5: Understanding Consequences
EJ-6: Reflecting on the Process and Outcome
EJ-7: Coping

Intro to the EthEx Model

SIX CONCEPTUAL STAGES ABOUT COOPERATION
AND THEIR CHARACTERISTICS
(From Rest, 1979)

PRECONVENTIONAL LEVEL

Stage 1: The ethicality of obedience: Do what you are told.
• Right and wrong are defined simply in terms of obedience to fixed rules.
• Punishment inevitably follows disobedience, and anyone who is punished must have been bad.
Example: Follow class rules to avoid detention.

Stage 2: The ethicality of instrumental egoism: Let's make a deal.
• An act is right if it serves an individual's desires and interests.
• One should obey the law only if it is prudent to do so.
• Cooperative interaction is based on simple exchange.
Example: Do chores to get allowance.

CONVENTIONAL LEVEL

Stage 3: The ethicality of interpersonal concordance: Be considerate, nice and kind, and you'll make friends.
• An act is good if it is based on a prosocial motive.
• Being ethical implies concern for the other's approval.
Example: Share your gum with the class and people will find you likeable.

Stage 4: The ethicality of law and duty to the social order: Everyone in society is obligated to and protected by the law.
• Right is defined by categorical rules, binding on all, that fix shared expectations, thereby providing a basis for social order.
• Values are derived from and subordinated to the social order and maintenance of law.
• Respect for delegated authority is part of one's obligations to society.
Example: Obey traffic lights because it's the law.

POSTCONVENTIONAL

Stage 5: The ethicality of consensus-building procedures: You are obligated by the arrangements that are agreed to by due process procedures.
• Ethical obligation derives from voluntary commitments of society's members to cooperate.
• Procedures exist for selecting laws that maximize welfare as discerned in the majority will.
• Basic rights are preconditions to social obligations.
Example: Obey traffic lights because they are designed to keep us all safe.

Stage 6: The ethicality of non-arbitrary social cooperation: How rational and impartial people would organize cooperation defines ethicality.
• Ethical judgments are ultimately justified by principles of ideal cooperation.
• Individuals each have an equal claim to benefit from the governing principles of cooperation.
Example: Everyone agrees that traffic lights keep us safe and so they will obey them for the common good.

Process 3: Ethical Motivation

Prioritizing the ethical action over other goals and needs
(either in the particular situation, or as a habit).

Following Mr. Anderson's decision about which action is most ethical, he must be motivated to prioritize that action, that is, be ethically motivated. Ethical motivation can be viewed in two ways, as situation-specific and as situation-general. Situation-general motivation concerns the day-to-day attitudes about getting along with others. It is a positive attitude towards ethical action that one maintains day to day. Blasi (1984) and Damon (1984) argue that self-concept has a great deal to do with ethical motivation generally, including attending to professional ethical codes. For instance, if one has a concept that one is an ethical person, one is more likely to prioritize ethical behaviors. Situation-specific ethical motivation concerns the prioritization of the ethical action choice in a particular situation. If all goes well, matching one's professional and personal priorities with possible actions results in ethical motivation, prioritizing the ethical action.

Ethical Motivation

Value identification
What are the values of my family/religion/culture/community? How should these values influence what is decided? How does each possible option fit with these values?

Prioritize the action
Am I willing to forego the benefits of NOT taking this best action?

Ethical motivation means that the person has placed the ethical course of action—which was selected in the process of ethical judgment— at the top of the list of action priorities. In other words, all other competing actions, values and concerns are set aside so that the ethical action can be completed. In other words, does a teacher put aside another priority at the moment, such as taking a break, in order to take an ethical action, such as stopping one student from insulting another? In our situation with Mr. Anderson, in order to continue along the route to completing an ethical action, he would have to put aside any other priority (such as teaching the lesson) and focus on performing the ethical action.

ETHICAL MOTIVATION SKILLS
EM-1: Respecting Others
EM-2: Cultivating Conscience
EM-3: Acting Responsibly

EM-4: Being a Community Member
EM-5: Finding Meaning in Life
EM-6: Valuing Traditions and Institutions
EM-7: Developing Ethical Identity and Integrity

Process 4: Ethical Action

*Implementing the ethical action by knowing how to do so
and following through despite hardship.*

Once Mr. Anderson has determined his priorities, he must complete the action and this requires ethical action. Ethical action involves two aspects: ego strength, the ability to persevere despite obstacles and opposition, and implementation skills, knowing what steps to take in order to complete the ethical action.

Ethical Action

Judge the feasibility of the chosen option
What is my attitude about taking this action? Do I believe it is possible for me to take this action? Do I believe that it is likely I will succeed?

Take action
What steps need to be taken to complete the action? Whose help do I need in my family/community/affiliative group? What back up plan do I have if this doesn't work?

Follow through
How do I help myself follow through on this action? How can others help me follow through? How do I resist giving up? How do I muster the courage to do it?

Reflect
What were the consequences of my decision? How did the decision affect me/my family/community/affiliative groups? Did the results turn out as I planned? In the future, should I change the decision or the decision process?

In our situation, Mr. Anderson might be very tired and have to draw up his strength and energize himself in order to take action. The implementation skills required in our scenario might include the manner of Mr. Anderson's intervention (e.g., severe and degrading reprimand versus a kind but firm reproach; or a culturally-sensitive approach that saves a student's 'face').

Let us consider another example. Perhaps a teacher knows that one of her students is smoking when he goes to the lavatory and she believes that it is best to stop him. Ethical action means that she has the action or fortitude to complete the ethical course of action. Many obstacles can arise to circumvent taking the ethical action. For example, if the student is 6 1/2 feet tall, she may feel physically threatened by the thought of confronting him and not even try. On the other hand, she may or may not know what steps to take to handle the situation. For example, to overcome fear for personal safety, she could ask another (bigger) teacher to help her or may inform the head of the school.

ETHICAL ACTION SKILLS
EA-1: Resolving Conflicts and Problems
EA-2: Asserting Respectfully
EA-3: Taking Initiative as a Leader
EA-4: Planning to Implement Decisions
EA-5: Cultivating Courage
EA-6: Persevering
EA-7: Working Hard

Need for All the Processes

These processes—ethical sensitivity, ethical judgment, ethical motivation, and ethical action—comprise the minimal amount of psychological processing that must occur for an ethical behavior to result. They are highly interdependent. That is, all the processes must be successfully completed before ethical behavior takes place. If one process fails, ethical action will not occur. For instance, if a teacher is highly sensitive to her students and environment but makes poor decisions (e.g., bargaining with students for their cooperation each day), poor outcomes may result. Or, a teacher may be sensitive to the situation, make a responsible ethical judgment, be highly motivated, but lack the backbone to follow through when a student challenges his action.

The processes also interact. That is, one may be so focused on one of the processes that it affects another process. For instance, the teacher who fears for her own safety or who values peace within the classroom may not challenge the students but try to keep them happy by not confronting any miscreant behaviors. Or, a teacher who is extremely tired and wanting to go home to rest may also be less sensitive to the needs of his students and miss cues that indicate ethical conflict.

Teaching Students Ethical Skills

The four-process model outlined here is helpful when thinking about designing instruction to promote ethical behavior. Like teachers, students face ethical dilemmas and situations each day. They have countless opportunities to demonstrate civic and ethical behavior. Their responses may be thoughtful and considerate or may be thoughtless and harmful to self and others. The teacher has a unique opportunity to help students nurture thoughtfulness and consideration of others. Our framework is intended to provide goals for teachers to do so. Our guide booklets suggest methods for reaching these goals during regular instruction.

We parcel each of the four processes into skills. The categorization of skills is not exhaustive but consists of skills that can be taught in a public school classroom. (There are other aspects of the processes that are either controversial or difficult to implement and assess in the public school classroom.) On the next page, we list the whole set of skills that are discussed in the guide booklets.

Ethical Behavior Skills for the Ethical Process Model

Activity Booklet 1: ETHICAL SENSITIVITY
ES-1: Understanding Emotional Expression
ES-2: Taking the Perspective of Others
ES-3: Connecting to Others
ES-4: Responding to Diversity
ES-5: Controlling Social Bias
ES-6: Interpreting Situations
ES-7: Communicating Well

Activity Booklet 2: ETHICAL JUDGMENT
EJ-1: Reasoning Generally
EJ-2: Reasoning Ethically
EJ-3: Understanding Ethical Problems
EJ-4: Using Codes and Identifying Judgment Criteria
EJ-5: Understanding Consequences
EJ-6: Reflecting on the Process and Outcome
EJ-7: Coping

Activity Booklet 3: ETHICAL MOTIVATION
EM-1: Respecting Others
EM-2: Cultivating Conscience
EM-3: Acting Responsibly
EM-4: Being a Community Member
EM-5: Finding Meaning in Life
EM-6: Valuing Traditions and Institutions
EM-7: Developing Ethical Identity and Integrity

Activity Booklet 4: ETHICAL ACTION
EA-1: Resolving Conflicts and Problems
EA-2: Asserting Respectfully
EA-3: Taking Initiative as a Leader
EA-4: Planning to Implement Decisions
EA-5: Cultivating Courage
EA-6: Persevering
EA-7: Working Hard

How Should Character Be Taught?
Development Through Levels of Expertise

Each process of the Ethical Expertise Model is divided into several skills. The skills in each process include elements that we think are fundamental and have aspects that can be taught.

We present the skills in terms of expertise development. Think about how a young child learns to talk. First the child is exposed to sounds of all sorts, rather quickly learning the specialness of speech sounds in the environment. The child begins to make sounds, later to mimic and have mock conversations with a responsive caregiver. After many months, an actual word is spoken. From there, the child adds to his or her vocabulary little by little and then in floods. Think of how many hours a child has heard speech before age 2. Think of how much there is to learn yet after age 2. There are many phases of development in language acquisition and mastery. These phases (or levels) are movements toward expertise—toward the eloquence of an Eleanor Roosevelt or William F. Buckley, Jr. We use the notion of expertise in making recommendations for instruction.

Why Use an Expertise Approach?

Billy has an IQ of 121 on a standardized individual intelligence test; Jimmy has an IQ of 94 on the same test. What do each of these scores, and the difference between them, mean? The ... best available answer to this question is quite different from the one that is conventionally offered—that the scores and the difference between them reflect not some largely inborn, relatively fixed ability construct, but rather a construct of developing expertise. I refer to the expertise that all of these assessments measure as developing rather than as developed because expertise is typically not at an end state but is in a process of continual development. (Sternberg, 1998, p. 11)

Current understanding of knowledge acquisition adopts the construct of novice-to-expert learning. According to this paradigm, individuals build their knowledge over time during the course of experience related to the knowledge domain. Robert Sternberg is a world-renown expert on human abilities and cognition who contends that abilities are developing expertise. Standardized tests measure how much expertise you've developed in a particular subject area or domain (and how much expertise you have at taking such tests).

In general, what do experts have that novices do not have?
Here is a list that Sternberg (1998) garners from research.
- Experts have large, rich, organized networks of concepts (schemas) containing a great deal of declarative knowledge about the domain
- Experts have well-organized, higher interconnected units of knowledge in the domain

What can experts do that novices cannot do?
Sternberg (1998) says that experts can:

- Develop sophisticated representations of domain problems based on structural similarities
- Work forward from given information to implement strategies for finding unknowns in problem solving
- Choose a strategy based on elaborate schemas for problem solving
- Use automated sequences of steps in problem solving
- Demonstrate highly efficient problem solving
- Accurately predict the difficulty of solving certain problems
- Carefully monitor their own problem-solving strategies and process
- Demonstrate high accuracy in reaching appropriate solutions to problems

The level of expertise described by Sternberg requires extensive study and deliberate practice. In primary and secondary schooling, there are many subjects to be covered and little time to spend on each one. Nevertheless, teachers can approach the subject matter as a domain of knowledge that novices can, over time, learn to master. Nurturing mastery of a domain is a lifelong endeavor. Teachers have a chance to help students develop the attitudes and motivation to monitor their own progress toward expertise.

How can novices develop expertise?
Sternberg (1998) suggests that novices should:

- Receive direct instruction to build a knowledge base (lecture, tutoring)
- Engage in actual problem solving
- Engage in role modeling of expert behavior
- Think about problems in the domain and how to solve them
- Receive rewards for successful solution of domain problems

For each skill in a process, we have condensed the complex acquisition of expertise into five skill levels (a larger number would be unmanageable). The purpose of the levels is to give teachers an idea of what students need for developing the given skill, knowledge, or attitude, or what kinds of behavior exhibit a certain level of expertise development. The levels refer to phases of development as both a process (ways to learn a skill) and a product (skills learned). Within each level are many sublevels and supplementary skills that we have not attempted to name. Instead, we use terms that point to the broad processes of building expertise in the domain. The levels are cumulative, that is, each level builds on the previous level. Further, within each skill are many domains. To develop new skills in a domain, the individual circles back through the levels to develop expertise.

Novice-expert differences in the skill categories

Some skill categories are learned from infancy for most people, requiring little conscious effort. For example, *Reading and Expressing Emotion* comes about naturally as a part of learning to get along with others. However, not everyone learns these skills, or learns them well, and few learn them across cultural contexts. Therefore, we include these 'naturally-acquired' skills as areas for all to expand cross-culturally and for some to learn explicitly.

Other skill categories are not learned as a matter of course during childhood. Instead they require concentrated effort. For example, *Controlling Social Bias* does not come naturally to any human or human group. We include these 'studied' skills because they are critical for ethical behavior.

Breaking down the skill category

Although we have parsed the processes into skill categories, the skill categories themselves can be broken down further into sub-skills. <u>We encourage you and your team to do this as much as possible.</u> When you do this, consider what a novice (someone who knows nothing or very little) would need to learn.

On the next page is a brief description of each level of expertise.

Levels of Expertise of an Ethical Behavior Skill

LEVEL 1: IMMERSION IN EXAMPLES AND OPPORTUNITIES
Attend to the big picture, Learn to recognize basic patterns

The teacher plunges students into multiple, engaging activities. Students learn to recognize broad patterns in the domain (identification knowledge). They develop gradual awareness and recognition of elements in the domain.

LEVEL 2: ATTENTION TO FACTS AND SKILLS
Focus on detail and prototypical examples, Build knowledge

The teacher focuses the student's attention on the elemental concepts in the domain in order to build elaboration knowledge. Skills are gradually acquired through motivated, focused attention.

LEVEL 3: PRACTICE PROCEDURES
Set goals, Plan steps of problem solving, Practice skills

The teacher coaches the student and allows the student to try out many skills and ideas throughout the domain to build an understanding of how these relate and how best to solve problems in the domain (planning knowledge). Skills are developed through practice and exploration

LEVEL 4: INTEGRATE KNOWLEDGE AND PROCEDURES
Execute plans, Solve problems

The student finds numerous mentors and/or seeks out information to continue building concepts and skills. There is a gradual systematic integration and application of skills across many situations. The student learns how to take the steps in solving complex domain problems (execution knowledge).

Who Decides Which Values to Teach?
The community

We have presented a set of ethical skills selected according to what enables a person to get along ethically with others and to thrive as a human being. The skills are to be taught developmentally, helping students build expertise. But what do the ethical skills actually look like? For example, what does "respecting others" look like? If one were to travel around the world, the answer would vary. While respect itself is a value worldwide, each community has its own understanding of how it should look. For example, to show respect in some cultures, one speaks quietly and demurely with little eye contact. In other cultures, respect involves looking others in the eye and expressing one's opinions openly. Likewise, "communicating well" or "identifying consequences" can vary across communities. In other words, while in its essence an ethical skill is the same across contexts, it may look different. In the EthEx Model, students learn the different ways a skill appears in their community.

The EthEx Model project emphasizes the importance of embedding the skill categories in community cultural contexts. We encourage communities to be involved in the specific aspects of creating a curriculum for skill development. We hope that the actual day-to-day practice of the skills be determined on site, in the community. Students can gather information about the skill from the community (parents, elders) and bring back that information to the classroom. The teacher can tailor the classroom work to the local understanding of the skill. If there are many interpretations of the skills because of diverse families, this diversity is brought into the classroom by the students themselves.

The goal of any character education program is to build good community members, for it is in communities that students express their values, make ethical decisions, and take ethical action. To be an effective community member in the United States, students need skills for democratic citizenship. These skills are included in the list of ethical skills.

What Is the Student's Role?
To decide his or her own character

The student is not a passive trainee in an EthEx classroom. Through classroom posters and bookmarks, each student is encouraged to think about the following questions: "Who should I be? What should I become?" As teachers approach each skill, these are the questions that should be raised. The teacher can ask students about each skill category, "How do you want to be known?— as [a good communicator, a problem solver, a leader]?" Sometimes the teacher has to identify a particular adult that the student trusts and ask, "What would [so and so] want you to be?" Every day, students should feel empowered with the knowledge that they are creating their own characters with the decisions they make and the actions they take.

The EthEx Model includes both **skills for personal development** and **skills for getting along with others**. All skills are necessary for ethical personhood. The better one knows oneself, the better one can control and guide the self, and the better able one can interact respectfully with others. On the next page we list the skills and the primary focus of each one, which is either on the self or others.

Ethical Behavior Categories for Each Process

The categories are skills the individual needs to develop for reaching individual potential and skills for living a cooperative life with others.

Process Skills	Focus
ETHICAL SENSITIVITY	
ES-1: Understanding Emotional Expression	Self and Others
ES-2: Taking the Perspective of Others	Others
ES-3: Connecting to Others	Others
ES-4: Responding to Diversity	Self and Others
ES-5: Controlling Social Bias	Self
ES-6: Interpreting Situations	Self and Others
ES-7: Communicating Well	Self and Others
ETHICAL JUDGMENT	
EJ-1: Reasoning Generally	Self
EJ-2: Reasoning Ethically	Self
EJ-3: Understanding Ethical Problems	Self and Others
EJ-4: Using Codes and Identifying Judgment Criteria	Self
EJ-5: Understanding Consequences	Self and Others
EJ-6: Reflecting on the Process and Outcome	Self and Others
EJ-7: Coping	Self
ETHICAL MOTIVATION	
EM-1: Respecting Others	Others
EM-2: Cultivating Conscience	Self
EM-3: Acting Responsibly	Self and Others
EM-4: Being a Community Member	Others
EM-5: Finding Meaning in Life	Self and Others
EM-6: Valuing Traditions and Institutions	Self and Others
EM-7: Developing Ethical Identity and Integrity	Self
ETHICAL ACTION	
EA-1: Resolving Conflicts and Problems	Self and Others
EA-2: Asserting Respectfully	Self and Others
EA-3: Taking Initiative as a Leader	Self and Others
EA-4: Planning to Implement Decisions	Self and Others
EA-5: Cultivating Courage	Self and Others
EA-6: Persevering	Self and Others
EA-7: Working Hard	Self

When Should Character Be Taught?
During regular instruction

EthEx stresses the importance of embedding character education into regular, academic, and standards-based instruction. We believe that character education should not stand alone but be incorporated into the entire spectrum of education for students. Regardless of the curriculum, teachers can always raise issues of ethics in lessons.

The second section of this book offers suggestions on how to integrate character development into regular academic instruction. The suggestions in this book are for only one of four processes. We hope you pick up the other three books in order to promote skill development in all processes and skills.

Characteristics of the EthEx Model

Provides a concrete view of ethical behavior
described in What Should Be Taught? section (pp. 9-19)

Focuses on novice-to-expert skill building
described in How Should Character Be Taught? section (pp. 20-23)

Addresses community cultural contexts
described in Who Decides Which Values to Teach? section (p. 24)

Empowers the student
described in What Is the Student's Role? section (pp. 25-26)

Embeds character education into regular instruction
described in When Should Character Be Taught? section (p. 27)

Ethical Sensitivity
How Ethical Sensitivity Skills Fit with Virtues

SUBSKILL VIRTUE	ES-1 Emotional Expression	ES-2 Taking Persectives	ES-3 Connecting to Others	ES-4 Diversity	ES-5 Controlling Social Bias	ES-6 Interpret Situations	ES-7 Communic- ating Well
Altruism		*	*			*	
Citizenship		*			*	*	*
Civility			*				*
Commitment			*				
Compassion	*	*	*				
Cooperation			*	*	*		*
Courage							
Courtesy			*	*	*		*
Duty							
Fairness		*			*		
Faith			*				
Forbearance	*	*			*		
Foresight		*				*	
Forgiveness					*		
Friendship			*	*			*
Generosity		*	*				
Graciousness	*		*	*		*	*
Hard work							
Helpfulness		*	*			*	
Honesty	*		*				*
Honor							
Hopefulness						*	
Includes others		*	*	*	*	*	*
Justice		*			*		
Kindness	*		*				*
Lawfulness							
Loyalty			*	*			
Obedience							
Obligation							
Patience	*					*	*
Patriotism					*		
Persistence							
Personal Responsibility		*				*	
Politeness	*		*				*
Respect	*		*		*		*
Reverence			*				
Self-control	*						*
Self-sacrifice							
Social Responsibility		*		*	*	*	
Tolerance	*	*		*	*		
Trustworthiness			*				
Unselfishness		*					

Ethical Judgment
How Ethical Judgment Skills Fit with Virtues

SUBSKILL / VIRTUE	EJ-1 Reasoning Generally	EJ-2 Reasoning Ethically	EJ-3 Understand Problems	EJ-4 Using Codes	EJ-5 Conse-quences	EJ-6 Reflecting	EJ-7 Coping
Altruism		*		*		*	
Citizenship		*	*	*		*	
Civility		*		*		*	
Commitment		*		*	*	*	*
Compassion		*	*	*		*	
Cooperation		*				*	
Courage							
Courtesy		*		*		*	
Duty		*		*		*	
Faith		*		*		*	*
Fairness		*	*	*		*	
Forgiveness				*		*	
Friendship		*		*			
Forbearance		*		*		*	*
Foresight	*	*		*			
Generosity		*		*		*	
Graciousness				*			*
Hard work	*	*					
Helpfulness		*		*		*	
Honor		*		*		*	
Honesty		*		*		*	
Hopefulness							*
Includes others		*		*		*	
Justice		*	*	*		*	
Kindness		*		*		*	
Lawfulness		*	*	*		*	
Loyalty		*		*		*	
Obedience		*		*		*	
Obligation		*	*	*		*	
Patience	*				*		*
Patriotism		*		*		*	
Persistence	*						
Politeness				*			
Respect		*		*		*	*
Reverence		*		*		*	*
Personal Responsibility	*	*	*	*		*	
Social Responsibility		*	*	*	*	*	
Self-control					*		*
Self-sacrifice		*				*	
Tolerance		*		*		*	*
Trustworthiness							*
Unselfishness		*		*		*	

Ethical Motivation
How Ethical Motivation Skills Fit with Virtues

VIRTUE \ SUBSKILL	EM-1 Respecting Others	EM-2 Cultivating Conscience	EM-3 Acting Responsibly	EM-4 Community Member	EM-5 Finding Meaning	EM-6 Valuing Traditions	EM-7 Ethical Identity
Altruism				*	*		*
Citizenship	*	*	*	*		*	
Civility	*	*					*
Commitment		*	*	*	*	*	*
Compassion	*			*	*		*
Cooperation	*	*	*	*	*	*	
Courage		*		*	*		*
Courtesy	*						
Duty	*	*	*			*	
Faith				*	*		*
Fairness				*		*	
Forgiveness	*				*		
Friendship	*						
Forbearance	*	*		*			
Foresight	*		*		*	*	*
Generosity				*			*
Graciousness	*			*			
Hard work			*	*		*	
Helpfulness	*		*	*			
Honor		*	*		*	*	*
Honesty	*	*					
Hopefulness	*		*	*	*	*	*
Includes others	*			*		*	
Justice						*	
Kindness	*			*			*
Lawfulness		*	*			*	*
Loyalty		*	*			*	*
Obedience		*					
Obligation		*	*	*			
Patience	*		*	*	*	*	
Patriotism						*	
Persistence			*		*	*	*
Politeness	*			*			
Respect	*	*	*	*	*	*	*
Reverence	*	*	*	*	*	*	
Personal Responsibility	*	*	*			*	*
Social Responsibility	*		*	*		*	*
Self-control	*	*	*	*	*		*
Self-sacrifice		*		*			*
Tolerance	*	*	*	*		*	
Trustworthiness		*		*			*
Unselfishness	*	*	*	*	*		*

Ethical Action
How Ethical Action Skills Fit with Virtues

VIRTUE \ SUBSKILL	EA-1 Resolving Conflicts	EA-2 Assertive-ness	EA-3 Initiative as Leader	EA-4 Planning	EA-5 Cultivating Courage	EA-6 Persevering	EA-7 Working Hard
Altruism			*		*	*	
Citizenship	*		*	*	*	*	*
Civility	*	*				*	
Commitment	*	*	*	*	*	*	*
Compassion		*	*	*	*		*
Cooperation	*	*	*	*			*
Courage		*	*		*		
Courtesy	*	*					
Duty	*		*	*	*	*	*
Fairness	*				*		
Faith			*	*	*		*
Forbearance	*	*	*		*	*	*
Foresight	*	*	*				*
Forgiveness							
Friendship	*			*			
Generosity			*		*		
Graciousness							
Hard work		*	*	*	*	*	*
Helpfulness			*		*	*	*
Honesty		*	*	*			
Honor	*		*	*	*		*
Hopefulness	*	*					
Includes others	*		*	*			
Justice	*			*	*		*
Kindness							
Lawfulness			*	*			*
Loyalty			*	*			*
Obedience							*
Obligation	*		*	*			*
Patience	*	*	*			*	*
Patriotism			*	*	*		
Persistence	*	*	*		*	*	*
Personal Responsibility	*		*		*	*	*
Politeness		*		*			
Respect	*	*	*	*			
Reverence			*	*			
Self-control	*	*	*	*		*	*
Self-sacrifice			*		*	*	
Social Responsibility	*		*		*	*	*
Tolerance	*	*	*				
Trustworthiness		*	*				
Unselfishness	*		*	*	*		

References

Bebeau, M., Rest, J. R., & Narvaez, D. (1999). Beyond the promise: A framework for research in moral education. *Educational Researcher, 28*(4), 18-26.

Bellah, R., Madsen, R., Sullivan, W., Swidler, A., & Tipton, S. (1985). *Habits of the heart: Individualism and commitment in American life.* Berkeley: University of California Press.

Bergem, T. (1990). The teacher as moral agent. *Journal of Ethical Education, 19*(2), 88-100.

Blasi, A. (1984). Moral identity: Its role in moral functioning. In W. M. Kurtines & J. L. Gewirtz (Eds.), *Morality, moral behavior, and moral development* (pp. 128-139). New York: Wiley-Interscience.

Damon, W. (1984). Self-understanding and moral development from childhood to adolescence. In W. M. Kurtines & J. L. Gewirtz (Eds.), *Morality, moral behavior, and moral development* (pp. 109-127). New York: Wiley-Interscience.

Etzioni, A. (1994). *The spirit of community: The reinvention of American society.* New York: Simon & Schuster.

Faul, S. (1994). *Xenophobe's guide to the Americans.* London: Ravette.

Goodlad, J., Soder, R., & Sirotnik, K. (1990). *The moral dimensions of teaching.* San Francisco: Jossey-Bass.

Kohlberg, L. (1984). *The psychology of moral development.* New York: Harper & Row.

National Education Association. (1975). *Code of ethics of the education profession.* Retrieved February 5, 2009, from http://ethics.iit.edu/codes/coe/nat.edu.assoc.1975.html

Rest, J. R. (1979). *Development in judging moral issues.* Minneapolis: University of Minnesota Press.

Rest, J. R. (1983). Morality. In P. Mussen (Series Ed.), J. Flavell & E. Markham, (Volume Eds.), *Manual of child psychology: Vol. 3, Cognitive development* (pp. 556-269). New York: Wiley.

Rest, J. R. (1986). *Moral development: Advances in research and theory.* New York: Praeger.

Steinberg, L. (1996). *Beyond the classroom: Why school reform failed and what parents need to do.* New York: Simon and Schuster.

Sternberg, R. (1998). Abilities are forms of developing expertise. *Educational Researcher, 3*, 22-35.

Nurturing
Ethical
Sensitivity

Organization of Ethical Action Booklet

Overview Pages
Ethical Action skills and subskills

Skill Sections (7 skill sections in all—the *"meat"* of the booklet)
Skill Overview (see sample page below)
Subskills (see sample pages on p. 37)
      Activities
      Assessment hints
      Climate suggestions

Appendix
Guide for Lesson Planning
'Linking to the Community' Worksheet
Rubric Examples
Special Activities
Resources
Linking EA Skills to Search Institute Assets
References

Skill Overview Page

Skill Title

WHAT the skill is

WHY the skill is important

SUBSKILLS list

Persevering
Ethical Action 6

WHAT
Perseverance enables individuals to complete actions that are important to them and others. Without it, many ethical actions would fail at the sight of the first obstacle or difficulty.

WHY
Perseverance is important for the completion of an ethical action. Children can be successfully instructed to 'talk to themselves' about not doing something, and instructed on how to distract themselves from unwanted behavior. A form of self-talk to complete a task can be a useful technique to help one find the ego strength to complete an ethical action—at any age.

SUBSKILLS OVERVIEW
Be steadfast
Overcome obstacles
Build competence

EA-6 Developing Perseverance: Overview

Skill Name: Subskill Name
Side Header

Ethical Sensitivity Overview

Subskill Activities Page

Skill & Subskill NAME

Expert Example

**Subskill Activities
by Level of Expertise**
*(4 levels total,
usually spans 2-4 pages
per subskill)*

Persevering by Building Competence

Expert

Christopher Reeves (who played Superman in the movies) had an equestrian accident that left him a quadriplegic. He could have given up in life and stayed home quietly, but he became a spokesman for those with spinal injuries, traveling to speak about the importance of research in spinal injuries.

Ideas for Developing Skills

Level 1: Immersion in Examples and Opportunities
Attend to the big picture, Learn to recognize basic patterns

Study self-efficacy. Discuss how, for a particular field, small successes give a person confidence to keep trying and try harder things. Find examples in literature, television and movies, or in a particular subject area. ★

Level 2: Attention to Facts and Skills
Focus on detail and prototypical examples, Build knowledge

Self-talk. Find examples of and discuss how to 'cheerlead' for yourself in different situations. What behaviors help you do your best and reach excellence? (1) Students discuss self-talk and behaviors that help one persevere. (2) Students interview older students or adults about general behaviors. (3) Students interview adults in roles they admire or strive for in a particular field. ★

Level 3: Practice Procedures
Set goals, Plan steps of problem solving, Practice skills

Examples of pushing oneself in helping others. Students interview elders about their personal experiences of (1) how they persevered in trying to help others; (2) how they persevered in working towards a goal that helped humanity.

Level 4: Integrate Knowledge and Procedures
Execute Plans, Solve Problems

Self-help. Have students practice ways to coach oneself to reach excellence in skills like these for a particular subject area: Persistence in mental and physical ... ...pleting tasks without

EA-6 Developing Perseverance: Building competence

Assessment Hints

Building competence

Use multiple-choice, true-false, short answer, or essay tests to assess student's knowledge of strategies to push oneself.

Have students write reports, based on observations or interviews, of what they learned about pushing oneself.

**Skill Name:
Subskill Name**
Side Header

**Hints for
Assessment**

Skill Climate Page

Create a Climate to Persevere

Regularly discuss the importance of finishing a task, as a group or individual.

Regularly point out what would happen if people did not persevere until a job was done (e.g., the highway, a bridge, your house, your car) and how it would affect people around them.

Discuss the importance of persevering in meeting your responsibilities to others.

Sample Student Self Monitoring
Persevering

Be steadfast	
	I wait to reward myself until I've finished my work.
	I don't wait until the last minute to do my work.
	I lose control when I am angry. (NOT)
	I control my feelings of anger.
	I resist my impulses to disobey rules.

EA-6 Developing Perseverance: Climate

What you need to know for success in school

1. That attitudes affect behavior
2. That what you believe/think about affects your behavior
3. That you have some control over your attitudes
4. That learning anything requires commitment (decision to put your energies into a task)

**Suggestions for
Creating a Climate
to Develop Skill**

**Sample Self-Monitoring
Questions for Student**

Selections to Post in the Classroom
for Developing Skill

Ethical Processes & Skills
with Ethical Sensitivity Subskills

Activity Booklet 2: ETHICAL JUDGMENT
EJ-1   Reasoning Generally
EJ-2   Reasoning Ethically
EJ-3   Understanding Ethical Problems
EJ-4   Using Codes and Identifying Judgment
         Criteria
EJ-5   Understanding Consequences
EJ-6   Reflecting on the Process and Outcome
EJ-7   Coping

Activity Booklet 3: ETHICAL MOTIVATION
EM-1   Respecting Others
EM-2   Cultivating Conscience
EM-3   Acting Responsibly
EM-4   Being a Community Member
EM-5   Finding Meaning in Life
EM-6   Valuing Traditions and Institutions
EM-7   Developing Ethical Identity and Integrity

Activity Booklet 4: ETHICAL ACTION
EA-1   Resolving Conflicts and Problems
EA-2   Asserting Respectfully
EA-3   Taking Initiative as a Leader
EA-4   Planning to Implement Decisions
EA-5   Cultivating Courage
EA-6   Persevering
EA-7   Working Hard

Activity Booklet 1: ETHICAL SENSITIVITY

ES-1 Understanding Emotional Expression
Identify and express emotions
Finetune your emotions
Manage aggression

ES-2 Taking the Perspective of Others
Take an alternative perspective
Take a cultural perspective
Take a justice perspective

ES-3 Connecting to Others
Relate to others
Show care
Be a friend

ES-4 Responding to Diversity
Work with group and individual differences
Perceive diversity
Become multicultural

ES-5 Controlling Social Bias
Diagnose bias
Overcome bias
Nurture tolerance

ES-6 Interpreting Situations
Determine what is happening
Perceive morality
Respond creatively

ES-7 Communicating Well
Listen and speak
Communicate non-verbally and in alternative ways
Monitor communication

Ethical Sensitivity Overview

Ethical Sensitivity

Ethical Sensitivity is the empathic interpretation of a situation in determining who is involved, what actions to take, and what possible reactions and outcomes might ensue. This component is influenced by Ethical Motivation and Ethical Judgment.

Outline of Skills

ES-1: READING AND EXPRESSING EMOTION
Reading emotions involves identifying the needs and feelings of the self as well as others (intrapersonal and interpersonal skills). Important to getting along well with others are learning when and how to appropriately express emotion and managing aggression.

ES-2: TAKING THE PERSPECTIVES OF OTHERS
Perspective-taking involves exploring multiple perspectives of situations or events and requires extensive practice and experience. Students need to practice taking the perspective of someone in their own cultural group, people outside their cultural group, and people who less fortunate. Taking another perspective builds empathy and tolerance, and motivates one to make changes to benefit others.

ES-3: CONNECTING TO OTHERS
Connecting to others involves expanding the sense of self-concern to include others. It also involves developing a sense of connectedness to other people/groups, both globally and locally. A person who feels a sense of connection to others is more likely to make decisions and take actions that reflect care and concern for others. Students need to learn the skills of showing and friendship so that they can connect positively to others.

ES-4: RESPONDING TO DIVERSITY
Working with interpersonal and group differences involves understanding how cultural groups differ and how differences can lead to conflicts and misunderstandings. It is important to understand culture in its broadest sense, as any system of shared values, behaviors and expectations. This definition allows us to include "business culture," "school culture," "soccer culture," etc. Students should develop skills for multicultural living which include the ability to shift from using one culture code to using another.

ES-5: CONTROLLING SOCIAL BIAS
Controlling social bias involves understanding, identifying, and actively countering bias. It also means fostering the opposite of prejudice, tolerance. It is important to reflect on the nature of bias and how it comes about before attempting to control social bias. Bias is a part of human nature because we all naturally prefer familiar things and familiar ways of thinking. It takes conscious effort to rethink our personal habits of acting and speaking, but it can promote a more respectful, fair society.

ES-6: INTERPRETING SITUATIONS
Interpreting situations involves developing the creative skills used in generating multiple interpretations of a situation and multiple alternatives for dealing with it. It also means having the skills to counter normal pitfalls in intersocial interpretation. This is a critical step in any kind of problem solving. People often repeat the same mistakes because they respond automatically without considering another way to behave.

ES-7: COMMUNICATING WELL
Good communication involves skills in listening, speaking, writing, and non-verbal communication. The particular communication skills needed for an encounter can vary according to the social context of communication (one-on-one, small group, large group, peers, adults and authorities, strangers, younger children) and the cultural context (culture, male/female, school/work/home).

Ethical Sensitivity

WHAT

Given that a moral situation or dilemma exists (e.g., Should I turn in this wallet that I found? Should I hit the kid who just rammed his shoulder into mine in the hallway? Should I speak up when I'm offended at a racist or sexist joke made by a friend?), sensitivity involves perception and interpretation of the events and relationships in the situation. The most basic aspect of sensitivity is noticing the elements indicating that the ethical situation exists (for example, noticing sexist language). Ethical sensitivity includes being aware of all the people who may be affected by the situation and how they would be affected. Sensitivity skills also include using divergent thinking processes to generate multiple interpretations and alternative options as well as identifying the consequences of these alternatives.

WHY

The skills within ethical sensitivity facilitate three main functions: *acquiring* information about the ethical situation, *organizing* that information, and *interpreting* the information. The "information" can represent perceived events, perceived relationships, currently experienced emotions, background knowledge of events and relationships accessed from memory, and existing attitudes accessed from memory (Crick & Dodge, 1994; Le Doux, 1996; Narvaez, 1996). The processes identified below include mostly cognitive processes that can be taught in the classroom. Deeper, emotional skills such as empathy and compassion evolve as the students observe role modeling and have personal, reflective experiences.

Acquiring Information: Includes processes of perception and inference
> Reading and Expressing Emotions
> Perspective-taking

Organizing Information: Includes processes of critical thinking and reflection
> Caring by Connecting to Others
> Working with Interpersonal and Group Differences
> Controlling Social Bias

Using/Interpreting Information: Includes processes of divergent thinking and prediction
> Generating Interpretations and Options
> Identifying Consequences of Options

ROLE OF TEACHER/ADULT

Adults can help students develop ethical sensitivity skills by modeling sensitive communication and actions, verbalizing empathic and compassionate reactions whenever possible. Adults can also foster an emotionally "safe" environment, in which it is alright to share personal reactions, make mistakes, and try again. Gentle positive and negative feedback is helpful in guiding students' development.

TACKLING EXCUSES AND HANGUPS

Sometimes students will resist learning or taking action, giving excuses like the following. We offer suggestions about how to counteract these attitudes.

'Why should I bother about them?' (sense of superiority)
Discuss this as a general human bias that one must consciously control.

'Yup, I was right about those homeless people. They're just lazy.'
Discuss the human tendency to look only for confirming evidence of personal bias. Work on perspective-taking.

'I couldn't help it. I was so mad.'
Discuss or demonstrate the benefits of giving emotions a "cooling down period" and being objective.

'It's not my problem.'
Discuss human relatedness (ES-3) and ethical responsibility (EM-4).

'That looks/tastes/smells weird!'
Work on reducing fear of the unknown and difference. Discuss the realistic risks and benefits of learning about something new.

'It's just a TV show. I know it's not real.'
Discuss the harm of desensitization to violence and objectification of people.

'The consequences are too far in the future to concern me.' (This is especially pertinent to young people's attitudes toward drugs, alcohol.) Bring in guest speakers who had these thoughts/attitudes and then experienced the "far off" consequences. Encourage students to discuss issues with the speaker.

'The possible consequences will never happen to me.' (e.g., getting pregnant, being arrested for vandalism, other crimes.) Bring in guest speakers who had these thoughts/attitudes and then experienced the "unrealistic" consequences. Encourage students to discuss issues with the speaker.

'The possible consequences will never happen to him/her/them.'
Bring in guest speakers who had these thoughts/attitudes and then witnessed the "improbable" consequences occurring to another (e.g., killing a friend or stranger by driving drunk). Encourage students to discuss issues with the speaker and ask many questions.

'I have no choice—my friends are making me do this.'
Have students practice assertiveness skills: (1) Describe the situation that is upsetting, without blaming or getting emotional; (2) Tell other person your feelings; (3) Tell other person what you want him/her to change; (4) Tell other person how the change would make you feel.

'It's not my fault—person X is who you should blame!'
Counter with techniques to foster feelings of responsibility/accountability for one's own actions: (1) Discipline with immediate consequences and a given reason. (2) Help parents with discipline plans that include giving reasons to students when disciplined. (3) Discuss related dilemmas with slight variations.

'I can't change this situation so I won't try.'
Counter with inspirational examples of how others make a difference (e.g., Rosa Parks, or a local community member who has made a difference). Discuss how the student is more similar than different to this person. Emphasize how the student can make a difference.

Ethical Sensitivity Overview

TACKLING EXCUSES AND HANGUPS (continued)

'This situation is none of my concern.' (e.g., witnessing a fight or a crime)
Counter with citizenship activities, discussing the importance of concern for others in the community and outside of the community. Discuss the purpose of citizenship and its related responsibilities. Study exemplars of good citizenship.

'There's no time to think of other alternatives!'
Discuss (1) human tendencies to lose control (and do harm) when emotions are high, and (2) the importance of carefully and systematically thinking through a dilemma or problem and decision so others and yourself will not be harmed in the immediate or distant future.

'Why should their well-being be my concern?' (lack of positive regard for life)
Encourage a more positive regard for life and discuss in class people who have a healthy regard for life.

'It's not my responsibility to save the world!' (not seeing the value of human existence)
Counter with a discussion of the interconnectedness of us all and our ethical obligations to each other.

'Why should I help them? Nobody's ever done anything for me!' (pessimistic attitude resulting from negative life experience) Discuss the importance of optimism, and of overcoming obstacles.

'It's their own fault that they're in this mess...not mine.' (lack of empathic understanding of others) Foster a discussion of those who are empathic and how to help another in distress.

'I've got other things planned...I don't have time to help!' (having immediate needs that are in opposition to caring for others) Discuss the importance of weighing others' needs against our own, developing courtesy, meeting obligations, and showing generosity.

'Being a citizen of the U.S.A. means freedom to do what I want.'
Counter with examination and discussion of various forms of citizenship. Discuss the purpose of citizenship and its related responsibilities.

'This is stuff that adults do.'
Discuss examples of the positive and meaningful impact of young people on the world (e.g., dot-com companies, altruistic group leadership, etc.).

'This is the stuff that people in x-group do.'
Give counter examples to sex-typing, group typing.

'Other people will take care of it.'
Discuss this as a general human bias.

'I don't want to look like a fool in front of my classmates.'
Discuss counter examples of young people being seen as assertive, taking action for others and standing out.

'I'm afraid that my classmates might get back at me.' (This may come up especially if the peers are involved in unethical or illegal activities.) Discuss choices of peers, role models and the consequences.

'I don't like people in that group.'
Discuss the changing nature of group membership and feeling 'outside.'

'I can't do it.'
Discuss this as an obstacle to overcome.

Ethical Sensitivity
How Ethical Sensitivity Skills Fit with Virtues

SUBSKILL VIRTUE	ES-1 Emotional Expression	ES-2 Taking Perspectives	ES-3 Connecting to Others	ES-4 Diversity	ES-5 Controlling Social Bias	ES-6 Interpret Situations	ES-7 Communic- ating Well
Altruism		*	*			*	
Citizenship		*			*	*	*
Civility			*				*
Commitment			*				
Compassion	*	*	*				
Cooperation			*	*	*		*
Courage							
Courtesy			*	*	*		*
Duty							
Fairness		*			*		
Faith			*				
Forbearance	*	*			*		
Foresight		*				*	
Forgiveness					*		
Friendship			*	*			*
Generosity		*	*				
Graciousness	*		*	*		*	*
Hard work							
Helpfulness		*	*			*	
Honesty	*		*				*
Honor							
Hopefulness						*	
Includes others		*	*	*	*	*	*
Justice		*			*		
Kindness	*		*				*
Lawfulness							
Loyalty			*	*			
Obedience							
Obligation							
Patience	*					*	*
Patriotism					*		
Persistence							
Personal Responsibility		*				*	
Politeness	*		*				*
Respect	*		*		*		*
Reverence			*				
Self-control	*						*
Self-sacrifice							
Social Responsibility		*		*	*	*	
Tolerance	*	*		*	*		
Trustworthiness			*				
Unselfishness		*					

Ethical Sensitivity 1

Understanding Emotional Expression
(Share emotions)

WHAT
Reading emotions involves identifying the needs and feelings of the self as well as others (intrapersonal and interpersonal skills). Important to getting along well with others are learning when and how to appropriately express emotion and managing aggression.

WHY
Intrapersonal emotional skills help us to be more effective in acting upon empathy and in dealing with personal emotions in general. Interpersonal emotional skills allow us to identify and respond appropriately to the emotional cues of others (e.g., like noticing when others might need help or a sensitive response). Skills in both reading and expressing emotions are necessary for communication, particularly resolution of problems and conflicts.

> *Teachers can convey warmth/immediacy by*
> 1. Conveying support of students as human beings.
> 2. Conveying appreciation of students' cultures.
> 3. Making sure to include all students (and their backgrounds) when using the terms "we" & "us."

SUBSKILLS OVERVIEW
Identify and express emotions
    In verbal communication
    In facial expression and body language
    In text and other expressive domains (art, music)
Finetune your emotions
Manage aggression

Web Wise
Use these websites to get information for jigsaw activities: http://apahelpcenter.org; http://www.kidshealth.org
Surfing the Net with Kids has lots of links for kids' knowledge building: http://www.surfnetkids.com
http://nonverbal.ucsc.edu

Understanding Emotional Expression
by Identifying & Expressing Emotions

Actors who perform in live theater have to be very skilled in identifying emotions and portraying them with every part of their bodies. Unlike film acting, there is no room for mistakes or acting with only part of the body. Live theater actors must have extensive knowledge of how to express emotions verbally, facially, and physically (not to mention lighting and sets). In addition to acquiring the knowledge, they must practice and develop the acting skills to actually express the emotions successfully. A few of the expert live theater actors (i.e., have won awards for their performances) include **Walter Mathau, John Lithgow, Anne Bancroft,** and **Judith Ivey**.

Creative and Expert
Implementer
Real-Life Example

Ideas for Developing Skills

Level 1: Immersion in Examples and Opportunities
Attend to the big picture, Learn to recognize basic patterns

Identifying actors' emotional expression. Watch several excerpts from movies or television shows in which an actor is expressing a particular emotion, from the overt to the subtle. Have students identify which emotion is being expressed.

Processing emotions from real-life tragedies. Set up visits from veterans, judges, etc. to hear first-hand stories of how people are affected by tragic events. As a class, process the experience by reflecting on the emotions of all people involved. Assess journal entries graded with a rubric (see Appendix for sample rubric).

Knowing your own feelings. Give students a list of events that would cause emotional reactions they can relate to (like not being invited to a party, getting knocked down in the hallway, winning the lottery). Have them fill in how they would feel, how they would react, and what would result. See *Ready-to-use Social Skills Lessons & Activities*, by Begun (1995), for worksheets.

Knowing how your body reacts. Part of identifying one's own emotions is knowing how your body reacts physiologically when you are angry, sad, surprised, nervous, etc. Have students take a specific incident from a story or their own lives and write, talk, or draw about their body's reactions (how it feels, how it affects decision-making). Assess by grading with a rubric.

Seeing emotions in our surroundings. Ask students to take 5 minutes to look around the room and write down every expression of emotion they see. If they get stuck, suggest that they think about the expression involved in what T-shirt a person chooses to wear or in how they choose to decorate their folders. The goal is to identify many ways that people express the way they feel.

Starred ⭐ activities
within each subskill
go together!

Understanding Emotional Expression
by Identifying & Expressing Emotions

Ideas for Developing Skills

Level 1 (continued)

Recognizing variety in expression. Have students bring in expressive art or music from home or internet research. Let them organize the expressive art pieces into emotion categories to recognize many different ways of expressing a single emotion (with the understanding that more than one answer is "correct" as long as they can justify their sorting). Assess their sorting of new expressive artworks.

How do people express emotion in different domains? Have students study the ways emotion is expressed in a particular subject area or line of work. For artistic creative work such as poetry, painting, composing music, emotions are integrated into the work. For more technical creative work like math or science, emotions are integrated into motives and interests (e.g., what drives the researcher to work so hard). For physical labor, emotion may be used as a source for physical energy. (1) Students read about work in the domain and find examples of emotional expression. (2) Speakers from different lines of work visit to discuss how emotion plays a part in their work. (3) Students interview a person in a line of work that interests them about the role of emotion. Students report on their findings.

Level 2: Attention to Facts and Skills
Focus on detail and prototypical knowledge, Build knowledge

 Recognizing actors' methods for communicating emotion. Show students an excerpt of a movie or TV program and have them identify the emotions expressed by the characters, asking students to identify the methods actors use to make us believe they are experiencing particular emotions. Use a variety of genres such as teenage drama, family drama, and suspense. Assess with a new excerpt by having them identify emotions as well as the body and language cues that the actor used to portray the emotion.

Identifying emotions in the news. Have students identify newspaper stories that report emotional expression (directly or indirectly), e.g., domestic abuse. Discuss what clues and context information help us identify emotions in the situations the stories describe.

Identifying emotions on the internet. Have students identify ways that people express themselves on the internet (web, email) and what clues we can use to understand those types of expressions (as opposed to regular text or real life).

Evaluating emotions on the internet. Have students identify ways that people express themselves on the internet (web, email). Discuss which ways are appropriate/respectful.

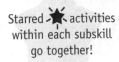
Starred ★ activities within each subskill go together!

Understanding Emotional Expression
by Identifying & Expressing Emotions

Ideas for Developing Skills

Level 2 (continued)

Journaling emotions. After reading or hearing a news story or historical account, have students reflect on their own reactions and emotions and then write about them. To focus their writing on expression (rather than the details of the story), ask them to describe the way they feel so that they could pick up the journal in 50 years and be able to feel the same emotion(s) just by reading their own entry. Assess with journal entries graded with a rubric (see Appendix for sample rubric).

Perspective-taking to understand effects of emotional expression.
To get better at expressing emotions, it helps for students to think about how others might react to their expressions. The best way for them to do this is to think about how they feel when people express emotions to them. Have the students finish sentences like, "When someone yells at me for something I didn't do, I feel _____." and "When someone tells me I did a good job on something, I feel _____."

Evaluating emotions in the news. Have students identify newspaper stories that report emotional expression (directly or indirectly), e.g., domestic abuse. Discuss whether the reported expression was appropriate or not, and what the people in the stories could have done differently.

What makes me feel? It is helpful to reflect on what triggers our emotions. Oftentimes it's the beliefs we carry that cause us to feel bad. Have students complete one or more of the following sections and then write about what they learned about themselves.
(1) *Worry*
    The things I worry about are...
    What I do when I get worried is...
    The beliefs I have that cause me to be worried are...
    Things I can do to change my worry to more positive feelings are...
(2) *Depression*
    What depresses me about school is...
    When I get depressed about school I...
    The beliefs I have that cause me to be depressed are...
    Things I can do to change my depression to more positive feelings are...
(3) *My future*
    The negative feelings I have about my future are...
    The things I do when I have those feelings are...
    The beliefs I have that cause those feelings are...
    Constructive attitudes I can adopt to change these feelings to more positive feelings are...

ES-1 Understanding Emotional Expression

Starred ✦ activities within each subskill go together!

Understanding Emotional Expression
by Identifying & Expressing Emotions

Ideas for Developing Skills

Level 3: Practice Procedures
Set goals, Plan steps of problem solving, Practice skills

Identifying and meeting others' social needs. Students practice identifying the needs of another person by reading their emotional cues. After viewing a video clip or reading an excerpt, ask students to guess what this person might need most (a kind word, help, to be left alone). This can also be an exercise in social creativity if the students focus on creating many possible ways of dealing with the situation.

Comparing emotional expression in different cultures. Provide several visual or auditory examples of the expression of the same emotion in different cultures. Discuss the human range of expression for several different emotions. (This may be tied to EM-1: Respecting Others and what level of expression a particular culture thinks is respectful.)

Noticing others' everyday expressions of emotions. Have students journal for a week on what feelings they notice most in others and what clues help them identify a certain feeling. The task could either focus on comparing the clues for different emotions or on comparing the ways that different people express emotions (i.e., comparing expression among family members versus friends). It might be helpful to set up a chart to help the students organize their observations.

Identifying emotions in negative situations. Have students generate different positive interpretations of situations where one is tempted to have a negative interpretation of the other person's emotional expression. Use situations like the following as well as those generated by students. For example: (1) your parent or friend yells at you for being late (a positive interpretation would be that they were worried about you); (2) your parent won't let you see a particular movie (a positive interpretation would be that they don't want you to get "hurt" in any way).

Role-playing emotion expression. Have students demonstrate expression of emotions in hypothetical dilemmas (such as feeling left out, wanting to talk to someone or to a group but being afraid of being laughed at, being angry that another student treats you unfairly, being angry that you've been punished unfairly by parents or a teacher, being afraid of going somewhere alone, being angry at someone who let you down). The rest of the class can try to guess the emotion being expressed. Assess by tracking participation or scoring each student's performance using a rubric (see Appendix for sample rubric).

Starred activities within each subskill go together!

Understanding Emotional Expression
by Identifying & Expressing Emotions

Ideas for Developing Skills

Level 3 (continued)

Break down steps in expressing emotion. (1) Pick a hypothetical or real example of an event that causes a positive emotion. Teach the following steps by having students follow the steps out loud in pairs or small groups, rotating the steps among the students. (2) As a follow-up, students can apply these skills to everyday situations and report or journal on how well the steps worked out for them.

1. Identify your feeling about the person or situation.
2. Identify exactly what it is about the person or situation that makes you feel that way.
3. Decide if the person or situation will benefit if you express your feelings.
4. Choose a time and place to express your feelings.
5. Anticipate response: How would you predict the other person would respond?
6. Express your feelings in a way that the other person will understand.

Level 4: Integrate Knowledge and Procedures
Execute plans, Solve problems

Predicting emotions. Read or watch a current event or fictional drama, stopping the story at a critical moment. Ask the students to predict the emotional reactions of the characters and how it will affect the outcome of  the situation. Assess by grading students' individual answers.

Using perspective-taking. Using current events, hypothetical dilemmas, or literary characters, have students take the perspectives of the characters in order to infer the emotions they are probably experiencing (may involve research). Have them role-play or write an essay or short story. Assess students' use of the following types of context information: personal, cultural, gender, age, socio-economic status, etc. (i.e., did their perspective-taking reflect consideration of these aspects?).

Starred ★ activities
within each subskill
go together!

Assessment Hints

Identify and Express Emotions

Essays. Students reflect on the emotions perceived and expressed in a video or TV show (to be shared and discussed with the class after individual papers are turned in).

Journaling. Over a period of time, students reflect on emotions expressed by themselves and the people around them.

Write a letter. The students write letters to express concern about an issue of importance to them.

Individual performance. Following a cooperative or class activity targeting a particular sensitivity skill, students are assessed on their individual performance using a new example.

Understanding Emotional Expression by Finetuning Your Emotions

Creative and Expert Implementer Real-Life Example

Through her professional experiences as a dancer, singer, actress, writer, poet, and film-director, **_Maya Angelou_** has become an expert at finetuning emotions. Ms. Angelou's books and poems have been bestsellers and won many awards. She is well known for connecting with her audiences in a powerful way.

Ideas for Developing Skills

Level 1: Immersion in Examples and Opportunities
Attend to the big picture, Learn to recognize basic patterns

Experimenting with drama and media. In a fun, relaxed atmosphere, allow students to improvise or follow loose scripts using various forms of performance media to experiment with expressing emotions. Consider music, prose, dance, visual art, and videography including lighting and sound effects. Assess by making each student personally responsible for one piece of a classroom production.

Emotional health. Discuss evidence of emotional health. Children experience all feelings. As they grow, they may be told not to express a particular feeling, but it is the nature of the body to express a feeling one way or another. There is nothing wrong with feelings; it's what you do with them that matters most.

What do people feel strongly about? People feel strongly about things that represent their values. For example, if you care deeply about the health of the planet, you might feel angry every time you see a sports utility vehicle (SUV) because it requires a lot of gasoline to run. (1) Students interview community leaders and members for the kinds of things they feel strongly about. Students should ask (a) Did you come to this conclusion after considering alternatives? What are the alternatives that you disagree with? What is the next best thing to your position if that one is not possible? (b) What are the consequences of your position? How does it affect other people and the planet? (c) How did you develop this belief? (d) Would you make your belief publicly known (e.g., by telling others, writing a letter to the editor of the newspaper)? (e) How have you acted on your value? (2) Students investigate famous people and how they express their values.

Understanding Emotional Expression by Finetuning Your Emotions

Ideas for Developing Skills

Level 1 (continued)

Appropriate human emotion.
(1) Basic feelings. Read stories in which one or more common human emotions are expressed. Then discuss the different types of basic feelings and what situations stimulate the feelings. See the chart under Post in the Classroom for different emotive words. (a) Feeling sadness. People feel sad when they lose something important, like a parent, a friend, a dream. People express this kind of grief in different ways. If a person feels desperately sad for more than a couple of weeks, they should get medical help. (b) Feeling joy. People feel joy when they are centered, when they feel connected to nature, when they feel unconditional love from another person, when they are doing work that they are passionate about. (c) Feeling anxiety. People feel anxious when the future seems uncertain, when unexpected things happen, and when they fail unexpect-edly. (d) Feeling afraid. People feel afraid when they feel threatened by physical harm or when a loved one is in danger.

(2) Identifying appropriate feelings. Give students a list of sentences and ask them to identify how the person probably feels. For example: John's dog just got hit by a car. Maria spends a day in the mountains. Abdul has a big test tomorrow that will decide his grade in the class. Leehoon hears a noise in the dark outside her house.

(3) Differences in feelings among families. Have students think about (perhaps observe for a few days) and describe the kind of feelings their families express and how. Some families are very expressive, expressing happiness, anger, sad-ness at a moment's notice. Other families are not very expressive at all or express only a few feelings (happiness but not anger).

Level 2: Attention to Facts and Skills
Focus on detail and prototypical knowledge, Build knowledge

Using different voice levels for different situations, different cultural contexts. (1) Ask students to sort the following situations into columns marked, "speak loudly" and "speak softly": talking to one or two people inside, talking to one or two people outside, talking to a large group inside, talking to a large group outside, giving a speech, presenting a report, telling someone you are angry, telling someone they hurt you, etc. There are no absolute right or wrong answers, but this activity can facilitate group or whole class discussion of all the things to consider. (2) Discuss cultural differences in ways that would be relevant for the students' everyday lives (if they interact with people from cultures in which people tend to speak loudly or softly). Also, talk about the potential for misunderstanding based on the volume and tone of one's voice.

Comparing writers' expression of emotions. Read several emotional pieces by writers (poems, journal entries, essays) and discuss similarities and differ-ences in how the emotions are being expressed.

Understanding Emotional Expression by Finetuning Your Emotions

Ideas for Developing Skills

Level 2 (continued)

What to do when you are feeling_____.
(1) Present examples from stories, films, scenarios of healthy ways that people express and manage feelings of anger, sadness, anxiety. For example, these could include:
- *Anger*: taking a deep breath and counting to 10, writing in a journal, talking to a friend or trusted adult about it
- *Sadness*: putting on relaxing music, writing in a journal, talking to a friend or trusted adult about it
- *Anxiety/fear*: telling a joke, writing in a journal, talking to a friend or trusted adult about it.

(2) Interview adults about what they do when they have a particular feeling.
(3) Interview counselors (e.g., ministers, psychologists) about what they tell people to do to identify their feelings and then manage them.
(4) What should I do? Have students select a way to try the next time they feel sad, or angry, or scared.

Feelings about yourself.
(1) Feelings about your body. Have students think about their feelings towards their bodies and what triggers positive and feelings (e.g., negative: media images, looking in the mirror; positive: putting on new clothes, dancing). Have students work on not taking in the negative messages and focusing on what triggers good feelings.
(2) Feelings about belonging. Have students list the situations in which they feel like they don't belong. Brainstorm on ways to counteract these feelings, including making changes in the classroom, and raising expectations on how students treat each other. Discuss the costs of belonging/not belonging. Point out that belonging can be good if it builds up your sense of worth and competence. Sometimes it's better not to belong a group that brings you down and makes you pessimistic about your future.

Level 3: Practice Procedures
Set goals, Plan steps of problem solving, Practice skills

Voicing social concern. Have students write a letter to express concern about some social or community issue (like trees being cut down on public property). Assess by grading letters with a rubric (see Appendix for sample rubric). If appropriate, send the letters.

Expressing sympathy. Have students write or say what they would say to a friend who just failed a test, lost a pet, didn't make the team, had a friend move away, or whose family is going through a divorce.

Understanding Emotional Expression by Finetuning Your Emotions

Ideas for Developing Skills

Level 3 (continued)

Fostering ethical emotions. Discuss ways to foster senses of fairness, compassion, and empathy—the moral emotions. Adopt one of these ways in the classroom.

Aligning feelings with obligations. Have students interview adults about how they taught themselves to want to meet their responsibilities or have students read stories about people who did this.

When do I feel what? Students should make lists of what makes them feel certain ways and then avoid those situations for bad feelings or seek them out for good feelings.

    I feel sad when.... (I don't get to talk to my Mom for a couple of days)

    I feel angry when....(my brother uses my computer without asking permission)

    I feel lonely when...(I don't get a date)

    I feel shame when...(I get a bad grade)

    I feel scared when...(I hear gunshots in the neighborhood)

    I feel hurt when...(my classmates make fun of me)

    I am deeply happy when...(I spend time with my best friend)

    I feel proud when...(my little sister says another new word)

    I feel hopeful when...(vacation comes)

Level 4: Integrate Knowledge and Procedures
Execute plans, Solve problems

Interpersonal conflict role plays. In pairs, the students role play a conflict in which both parties equally are at fault (for example, a miscommunication or forgetting to do something). Focus on the higher-level tasks of anticipating the other person's reaction and choosing words/actions that reflect that perspective taking. Assess role plays using a rubric (see Appendix for sample rubric).

Critiquing emotion expression. Have students think critically about ways to express emotion. For example, expand the role play or writing assignment to include at least two strategies/approaches for expressing the emotion as well as a critique of the different approaches, selecting the one that seems the most constructive. Assess by grading on how well the student follows the process of considering several strategies and then selecting one (see Appendix for sample rubric).

Writing with emotional sensitivity. Have students write a short story that conveys different emotions (in the same or different characters).

Understanding Emotional Expression by Finetuning Your Emotions

Ideas for Developing Skills

Level 4 (continued)

Expression during a service learning or community project. Have a community member rate students on their emotional expression.

Media with the wrong messages. Some media (e.g., movies) tell stories in such a way as to decrease ethical responses. For example, people who watch a lot of "slasher" movies have less empathy for victims of rape. Some shows suggest that violence is an appropriate way to deal with conflict and many programs or movies show few negative consequences of violence. Have students identify television shows or movies that go too far in disrespecting human life. Then write a letter of complaint to the movie studio who created the film, to the network who showed it, and to the advertisers who sponsored it.

Assessment Hints

Finetune Your Emotions

Reflective essays. Students reflect on their emotions perceived and expressed in a journal/diary that they keep.

Role plays. Have students role play emotional states verbally and nonverbally.

Acting. Have students read a role or part in an appropriate manner.

Understanding Emotional Expression by Managing Aggression

In the 1960s, **Cesar Chavez** organized a strike-boycott against the Carlifornia grape growers in order to express his outrage with the conditions that migrant farmers had to work under. Mr. Chavez led a successful five-year strike-boycott that attracted millions of supporters to the United Farm Workers union. He brought together unions, church groups, students, minorities, and consumers to support his cause.

Creative and Expert Implementer Real-Life Example

Ideas for Developing Skills

Level 1: Immersion in Examples and Opportunities
Attend to the big picture, Learn to recognize basic patterns

Trigger points. Students construct an interview or survey asking people to identify personal trigger points that make them angry and particular examples of when they were triggered. Students discuss how trigger points can affect communication.

Controlling anger. Students interview older students and adults about how they control their anger. Class discusses methods of controlling one's anger.

Awareness of own reactions. Watch film/video clips and discuss how the characters handled their feelings. Were they self-aware? Have students practice and keep a journal on: (1) Knowing their feelings. (2) Stopping and thinking before acting on strong feelings.

Know about anger. People feel angry when they don't get something they want or think they deserve (e.g., respect, being treated fairly). Anger is usually not helpful because it narrows our focus and highlights negative feeling. It makes us frustrated and less likely to take constructive action to solve problems. It makes us want to punish others and demand our way.

What does aggression look like? Discuss examples of psychological aggression (ranging from direct aggression like bullying or sarcastic remarks to indirect aggression like gossip, slander, or cold shoulders) and of physical aggression (e.g., pushing, pinching, tripping, hitting). Ask students to observe the behavior of others for a week and tally how much of each they see.

How to tell you are feeling aggressive. When you are angry, you are likely to feel (based on information from http://apahelpcenter.org): tense muscles (e.g., jaw and fists), rapid heartbeat, breathing changes, pain in your abdomen, shaking, flushed, goose bumps. Ask them to monitor their own behavior for these signs and keep track in a diary.

"It was during those long and lonely years that my hunger for the freedom of my own people became a hunger for the freedom of all people, white and black. I knew as well as I knew anything that the oppressor must be liberated just as surely as the oppressed. A man who takes away another man's freedom is a prisoner of hatred, he is locked behind the bars of prejudice and narrowmindedness. I am not truly free if I am taking away someone else's freedom, just as surely as I am not free when my freedom is taken from me. The oppressed and the oppressor alike are robbed of their humanity."
Nelson Mandela, *Mandela: An Illustrated Autobiography*, p. 202.

Understanding Emotional Expression by Managing Aggression

Ideas for Developing Skills

Level 1 (continued)

(1) <u>Ask the elders.</u> Interview elders about the ways they deal with anger without resorting to violence. Do the elders talk about their feelings with someone? Do they express their disappointment or displeasure calmly? Do they try to understand the other person's point of view when they are being criticized? Do they negotiate to work out solutions to problems with others? (2) <u>Activists.</u> Investigate the lives of activists and peacemakers to find out their techniques for managing anger and aggression.

Level 2: Attention to Facts and Skills
Focus on detail and prototypical examples, Build knowledge

Controlling aggression against others. Discuss practicing self-control of anger and aggression against others for a week and how one might use one's aggressive energies elsewhere. Students watch themselves and practice for a week keeping a journal. Provide a list of information for each situation written about. Assess journal entries using these guidelines.

Respectful expressions of negative emotions. Discuss differences between respectful and disrespectful emotional expression of anger, irritation, distress, etc. in different situations by acting out some different ways one can express frustration with a customer service representative, or a parent, or a peer, or a teacher, etc.

Does masculinity require aggression? Discuss and investigate the nature of masculinity. Is aggression a necessary characteristic? Does the practice of "letting boys be boys" ever go too far? Where should the line be drawn? Where does harm begin? Who gets to decide? How should we expect boys and girls to act in our classroom?

Managing provocation. Novaco (1975) suggests several steps to take in self-talk in order to manage a provocation successfully. Have students role play these in response to someone balling them out. (1) When possible, be prepared for a provocation ("This could be bad, but I can handle it." "I know what to do if I start to get upset."). (2) Experience the provocation "I am in control as long as I keep my cool." "I don't need to prove myself."). (3) Cope with arousal and agitation ("My anger tells me that I should start coaching myself to stay cool." "It's not worth losing my temper."). (4) Reflect on the experience and engage in self-reward for coping successfully ("I did a good job keeping my cool." "I get better and better at handling my anger.").

Understanding Emotional Expression by Managing Aggression

Ideas for Developing Skills

Level 2 (continued)

What precedes aggression?

(1) <u>Video examples.</u> Present or have students find examples of aggression from television and magazines. Discuss what sparked the aggression and what alternative actions were possible.

(2) <u>External threat.</u> People can respond with aggression to things that appear threatening. People feel threatened by cues related to physical harm (such as loud noises, being grabbed from behind), cues that appear punishing or non-rewarding, cues that remind them of previous situations in which harm occurred, cues that remind them of scary movies, cues that make things seem out of control, and even stimuli that are novel. People who grow up in angry environments are more likely to see threat when there isn't any. If you are one of these people, you must learn to check out your perspective with trustworthy others.

(3) <u>Individual reasons.</u> Discuss the following reasons that people use violence. Have students find examples of each in literature and other media. People use violence (a) in order to release feelings of anger or frustration, as they think that there is no other way to respond; (b) in order to manipulate or control other people (e.g., domestic violence); (c) in order to retaliate for harm done to them or loved ones; (d) in order to fill a need for attention; (e) becausye they have easy access to weapons; (f) because of peer pressure; (g) because they were abused as children; (h) because they see violence in real-life or in the media (the "mere exposure effect").

What makes me angry? Based on *Reaching Out* (Johnson, 1986)
Have students work alone to complete the following sentences with as much as they can say. Then they can reflect in a journal about what they might do to alleviate some of the causes of anger or they can meet in groups to discuss this.

(1) <u>In general.</u>
    The things I get angry about are...
    What I do when I get angry is...
    The beliefs I have that cause me to be angry are...
    Things I can do to change my anger to more positive feelings are...

(2) <u>Relationships.</u> The questions can address friends (as written), classmates, or other relationships.
    I feel angry when my friends...
    When I am angry at my friends, I usually...
    After expressing my anger at my friends, I feel...
    The way I express my anger at my friends makes them feel...
    When I feel that way, I usually...
    After reacting to my friends' anger, I feel...
    My reactions to my friends' anger usually results in their...

Understanding Emotional Expression by Managing Aggression

Ideas for Developing Skills

Level 2 (continued)

Use your anger to attack real problems. Anger can be a rational reaction to real problems in life. This kind of anger is healthy and can provide the energy to handle the problem. It is important to make a doable plan for change but then to keep in mind that maybe the problem can't be resolved right away (or ever) and that you need to manage your response to it instead (e.g., using relaxation techniques). Have students discuss situations like the following. Virginia Ramirez relates what happened when she heard that an old woman in her neighborhood had died in the cold:

> *I didn't know what to do. It was very hard to control my anger. I'd kept it quiet for so many years that when I began to let it out, it consumed me. When I first spoke out I bit people's heads off. I had to do role-playing to learn how to have an impact without attacking people. You lose control when you feel there's nothing you can do. When you feel you can stop these bad situations, you do it in a different way. I'll always be angry about the situation of my community....If I can work for the long run, I'll have better results.* (quoted in Loeb, 1999, pp. 323-324).

Long-term or extreme aggression. Sometimes children are in situations that are abusive. These are situations that need to be dealt with right away. (1) Find information on the web about abuse and crises (see list below) and use in a jigsaw activity (see appendix for description). (2) Discuss and design emergency plans with the students and give students phone numbers to dial and websites to access. Adults should help students figure out which adults they can trust to help them, and what to do in particular situations.

Eating Disorders Help Line	1-800-382-2832 (24 hrs)
Domestic Abuse/Assault	1-800-333-SAFE (24 hrs)
Teen AIDS Line	1-800-234-TEEN (M-F) 800-440-TEEN (weekends)
National AIDS Line	1- 800-342-AIDS
Nat'l Teen Gay & Lesbian Hotline	1-800-347-TEEN (Thurs.-Sun., 7 pm-11:45 pm ET)
Family/Children's Mental Health	1-800-654-1247 (24 hrs)
National STD Hotline	1-800-227-8922 (24 hrs)
Child help - Child Abuse Reporting	1-800/4-A-CHILD (24 hrs)
Family Violence Help Line	1-800/222-2000 (24 hrs)
National Runaway Hot Line	1-800-HIT-HOME (24 hrs)
Runaway Help Line	1-800-621-4000 (24 hrs)
Covenant House Crisis Support	1-800-999-9999 (24 hrs)
Suicide Help Line	1-800-SUICIDE (1-800-784-2433)
Youth Crisis Line	1-800-448-4663
RAINN - Rape Support Line	1-800-656-HOPE
Pregnancy Support and Advice	1-888-4-OPTIONS
General Crisis Counselling	1-800-785-8111

ES-1 Understanding Emotional Expression

Understanding Emotional Expression by Managing Aggression

Ideas for Developing Skills

Level 3: Practice Procedures
Set goals, Plan steps of problem solving, Practice skills

Quick options in an emotional situation. We don't always have time to sit down and rationally think out the best way to express an emotion. This is especially hard when someone says something to our face that makes us feel hurt or angry. We often feel compelled to act immediately. Lead the students through a discussion of how to appropriately express hurt or anger as an immediate reaction. Let them practice responding in role plays or essays to someone calling them a name, someone cutting them in line, someone running into them in the hallway and making them drop something, etc. Assess by grading their participation or with a short answer test on what they can do or say in these situations.

Dealing constructively with someone angry at you (Gibbs, Potter, & Goldstein, 1995). Have students practice the following steps. (1) Listen to the other person with an open mind. Try not to be defensive. Ask questions to find out what you did that upset the other person. (2) Find something that you can agree with in what the person says. Tell the person that you understand that the person is angry. Tell the person that it's understandable and they have a right to be angry. (3) Apologize or explain why you acted the way you did. Make a constructive suggestion about how to make things right. Examples of situations to role play: (a) Your parent or guardian is angry at you for leaving a mess in the kitchen. (b) The teacher is angry that you were disruptive in class. (c) A friend is angry because you called him or her a name.

Using your imagination to sidestep aggression directed at you. (Inspired by Hendricks & Wills, 1975). After practicing the following techniques, role play situations where one person directs hostility at another person. Have the 'victim' do one of the following. (a) Imagine the bad energy or words as a breeze going by. (b) Imagine it is a boomerang that you step aside from which returns to the sender. (c) Imagine you are wearing armor or slippery duck feathers and it bounces off. (d) Imagine it is snow that melts in the heat of your strength.

Express your anger constructively. Generally speaking, if you feel angry at someone: Tell them kindly directly, or let it go. The following is based on an exercise in Gibbs, Potter, and Goldstein (1995). Have students brainstorm a list of things that might make them angry and then have them practice the steps of telling someone in a constructive way. (1) Identify the problem and how you are feeling. (2) Plan what you will say, to whom, and when. When is a good time to bring it up? (3) State your complaint. Take responsibility for your part in the problem. (4) Make a constructive suggestion. (5) Reflect on how it went.

Understanding Emotional Expression by Managing Aggression

Ideas for Developing Skills

Level 3 (continued)

What to do when you feel angry.

(1) Don't attack the other person. Here is a list of things not to say accompanied by a better way (more respectful, direct and honest) to say them (adapted from Johnson, 1999).

DON'T SAY	DO SAY
A label: You are thoughtless and rude.	When you ignore what I say I get angry.
A command: Get lost!	Please leave, I need to work.
A question: What's wrong with you?	You are saying things that disturb me.
Accusations: You hate me!	Because you didn't invite me, I feel left out.
Sarcasm: That's great.	I'm mad because you forgot to bring our project.
Approval: You are terrific!	I really like you.
Disapproval: You are a terrible person.	I don't like you.
Name calling: Don't be a nerd.	You are making me feel embarrassed.

(2) Practice anger reduction. Have students practice methods for reducing the feelings of anger (e.g., fast heartbeat, fists and jaw clenching, rapid breathing) through mental conditioning: (a) Take several deep breaths, concentrating on breathing. (b) Imagine yourself someplace pleasant like at a beach. (c) Tell yourself to "relax" and that you don't need to prove anything. (d) Tell yourself that that you won't let it get to you, that you won't let your anger control you. (e) Tell yourself that the target of your anger is confused, innocent, or misguided. (f) Focus on solving the problem without making a scene and without targeting the other person. (g) Think about the benefits of controlling your anger. (h) Stop and consider the consequences of your actions.

(3) Practice changing your thinking. Have students practice mental moves that can keep their anger from escalating such as "reframing" or Cognitive Restructuring. This means changing your thinking. Sometimes when people feel emotional their thoughts are exaggerated and dramatic. Sometimes things go wrong but it doesn't mean the world is out to get you. You must learn to tell yourself that it is not the end of the world. Don't use words like "never" or "always" when talking about your life (e.g., "it never works" or "I always screw up") because they will prevent you from solving the problem and discourage others from helping you. Use logic in thinking about the situation. Change your firm expectations (I must have...) to desires (I would like to have....) and this will keep you from getting angry in the first place.

(4) Use your energy another way. Sublimate the anger when it is not appropriate to express it. Use physical exercise, private physical expression, deep relaxation or meditation, or detachment.

Understanding Emotional Expression by Managing Aggression

Ideas for Developing Skills

Level 4: Integrate Knowledge and Procedures
Execute plans, Solve problems

Recording aggression. Students each keep a record of their emotions. After a week they should identify any patterns such as trigger situations, lack of a repertoire of responses, etc. Make a class list of situations that are difficult for the students. Students should practice alternative ways of expression in those situations.

A community problem that makes you angry. Brainstorm on community problems and agree on one that the class feels strongly about changing. Use the steps suggested by Lewis, Espeland, and Pernu's (1998) *Kid's Guide to Social Action* (written for kids to use with worksheets and concrete guidelines): (1) Choose a problem in the neighborhood. (Does an area feel unsafe? Smell bad? Look terrible? Are there needy people?). (2) Do your research. (How do community members feel about the problem? What is the history of the problem?). (3) Brainstorm possible solutions and choose the one that seems most possible and will make the most difference. (4) Build coalitions of support. Find all the people that agree with you (neighborhood, community, city, state, businesses, agencies). (5) Figure out (with the help of your coalition) who is your opposition and work with them on overcoming their objections. (6) Advertise (send out a news release, call tv, radio, newspaper reporters, churches). (7) Raise money if you need to. (8) Carry out your solution. Make a list of the steps you need to take (e.g., write letters, give speeches, pass petitions). (9) Evaluate and reflect on whether the plan is working. Did you try everything? Should you change something? Celebrate what you have done by writing about it, dramatizing it, drawing it. (10) Don't give up. Find the thing that will work.

Assessment Hints

Manage aggression

Role play. Have students role play, keeping one's temper during provocation.

Journaling. Have students keep a dialogue journal (teacher writes back) about their own management of aggression. Or have students keep a journal on responses to literature and other readings involving aggression.

Essays. Have students write a reflective essay on personal awareness and growth of how to manage aggression.

Keeping a record. Have students keep a record of progress on their skill in managing aggression.

Create a Climate
to Understand Emotional Expression

To improve group interaction (from Lickona, 1992, p. 95).
Discuss discussing. Have the students write 2 things that others can do in a discussion that make you feel good and 2 things that make you feel bad. The students can share their lists in small groups. Then the class meets together to perform a "circle whip" in which each person tells a positive thing going around the circle and the same for a negative. Everyone keeps notes and at the end selects something to improve on.

To encourage the quiet children. When the class is used to some discussion but some students still aren't participating, perform a similar exercise to (1) Ask them to write down 2 things that help them participate in discussions and 2 things that keep them from discussing. (2) Then meet in small groups. (3) Instead of individual reports, have group reports about the positives and then the negatives. (4) The class should discuss how to make discussion comfortable for everyone. Encouraging quiet children through written communication. Teachers can be sensitive to shy students' inhibitions in speaking out in a group. To give these students an opportunity to express themselves, teachers can set up a box in which students can express an opinion or concern (either signed or anonymously). The teacher should read these daily and respond as quickly as possible.

Good thing/Bad thing. Practice emotion sharing by sharing one good thing and one bad thing that happened during the week.

Encourage the development of ethical emotions. Help students let go of negative emotions, unless they are a realistic response to injustice or abuse. Then help them use the energy to make change. Convey to students the importance of learning to control your temper. Convey to students that ethical feelings are important to cultivate: empathy, compassion, justice.

Sample Student Self-Monitoring
Understanding Emotional Expression
Encourage active learning by having students learn to monitor their own learning

Identify and Express Emotion

I understand that people express emotions differently.

I understand the different ways people express (sadness, anger, frustration, happiness, etc.) in my family/community/school/classroom.

There are times when it is important to know how someone else feels.

There are times when knowing how someone else feels is none of my business.

If I want to understand how someone is feeling, what do I need to pay attention to?

How do I express my own emotions?

How should I express my emotions if I want to make peace?

How should I express my emotions if I want to solve a problem that I am angry about?

How should I express my emotions if I want to make a friend?

How should I express my emotions if I want to help someone feel better?

How should I express my emotions if I want to be a role model?

Is it always right to tell someone exactly what you feel?

Finetune Emotion

I can identify my feelings in a given situation.

I accept my feelings as being part of me.

I express my feelings appropriately.

I have choices for how to react to anger.

I have choices for how to react to sadness.

I have choices for how to react to fear.

I know how to change my thinking to change my emotions.

I feel empathy for those who suffer.

I am careful to avoid desensitizing myself to the welfare of others.

I try to foster compassion for others in myself.

I avoid feeling envy or coveting what others have.

I do not nurture resentment in myself or others.

I value fairness for others.

I work on feeling positive about my responsibilities.

Manage Aggression

I control my temper when I have a conflict.

I know several choices I have when I get angry.

I understand that anger is usually based on irrational beliefs—that I should get my own way and that others should be punished for frustrating me.

I know how to minimize my irrational beliefs.

I can tell I am angry from the way my body feels.

I know what things can make me angry.

I can express my anger constructively.

I can let go of my anger after I express it constructively or use another technique to deal with it.

Selections to Post in the Classroom
for Understanding Emotional Expression

Happy words	Sad words	Confused words	Angry words	Fear words	Anxiety words	Embarrassment words
Amazed	Blue	Bewildered	Angry	Afraid	Anxious	Apologetic
Blissful	Crushed	Concerned	Annoyed	Alarmed	Exasperated	Ashamed
Delighted	Dejected	Confused	Betrayed	Apprehensive	Frustrated	Blameworthy
Eager	Depressed	Flustered	Bitter	Fearful	Hysterical	Degraded
Elated	Despairing	Frustrated	Cheated	Frightened	Insecure	Disrespected
Excited	Disappointed	Guilty	Disgusted	Hesitant	Jumpy	Embarrassed
Glad	Discouraged	Hesitant	Exasperated	Intimidated	Nervous	Foolish
Happy	Gloomy	Helpless	Furious	Isolated	Overwhelmed	Guilty
Joyful	Glum	Hopeless	Huffy	Nervous	Self-conscious	Humiliated
Pleasant	Hopeless	Numb	Ignored	Petrified	Threatened	Meek
Pleased	Hurt	Shocked	Irritated	Scared	Troubled	Mortified
Proud	Lost	Skeptical	Jealous	Shocked	Uneasy	Regretful
Relaxed	Miserable	Stuck	Mad	Stunned	Unsure	Repentant
Satisfied	Rejected	Surprised	Outraged	Timid	Vulnerable	Sorry
Wonderful	Sad	Torn	Persecuted	Trapped	Worried	Stupid
	Unhappy	Uncertain	Pressured			
	Upset	Uncomfortable	Resentful			
		Unsure	Tense			

Selections to Post in the Classroom
for Understanding Emotional Expression

Warning signs of aggression
(from www.apahelpcenter.org)

If you see these immediate warning signs, violence is a serious possibility.
* Losing one's temper daily
* Frequent physical fights
* Vandalism or property damage
* Increased use of drugs
* Increased risk-taking behavior
* Plans to commit acts of violence
* Announcing plans for hurting others
* Hurting animals
* Carrying a weapon

Ethical Sensitivity 2

Taking the Perspective of Others

(See like others)

WHAT

Perspective-taking involves exploring multiple perspectives of situations or events and requires extensive practice and experience. Students need to practice taking the perspective of someone in their own cultural group, people outside their cultural group, and people who less fortunate. Taking another perspective builds empathy and tolerance, and motivates one to make changes to benefit others.

WHY

The ability and habit of perspective-taking is important for developing skills in communication and problem-solving and is related to prosocial behaviors (Eisenberg & Mussen, 1989). We particularly need this skill to see both sides in a conflict, understand how our communication is perceived by others, and to develop empathic skills (starting with emotional perspective-taking).

SUBSKILLS OVERVIEW

Take an alternative perspective
Take a cultural perspective
Take a justice perspective

Web Wise

See the Multicultural Pavilion: http://www.edchange.org/multicultural
Equity issues at http://www.tcequity.org
www.rippleeffects.com has tools for taking perspectives

Take the Perspective of Others by Taking an Alternative Perspective

Pearl Buck was born in the United States but spent most of her first forty years in China. She wrote over seventy books. She was the first writer to bring the Asian perspective to Western literature. After she moved to the United States during the second half of her life, she was one of the most outspoken advocates for cross-cultural understanding between the United States and Asia.

Creative and Expert Implementer Real-Life Example

Ideas for Developing Skills

Level 1: Immersion in Examples and Opportunities
Attend to the big picture, Learn to recognize basic patterns

People can have different perspectives of the same thing. Have students make a chart of what is similar and different about people's responses to a particular experience. For example: a flavor test, a movie, a piece of clothing, a food, an activity, etc.

Stories of personal difficulty. Have students learn about other young people who have difficulties (e.g., kids their age who suddenly become quadriplegic, lose their homes or parents). These stories can be taken from a variety of resources including films, magazine stories, the internet, the news, history, etc.

Use drama and reading to take perspectives. Use dramatic reading of stories with dialogue or Reader's Theatre (scripts and worksheets available at http://www.stemnet.nf.ca/CITE/langrt.htm) with many resulting benefits. Afterwards, discuss the feelings and opinions of their character.

Level 2: Attention to Facts and Skills
Focus on detail and prototypical knowledge, Build knowledge

Communicating with multiple perspectives. (1) Have students write two descriptions of how to get to the bathroom (e.g., one using distances, the other using landmarks). (2) Have students give oral directions to a student on how to do a physical task. The one receiving directions is "handicapped" by being unable to use a part of his or her body (e.g., eyes, arms). (3) Have students communicate with one another using only gestures (no words). (4) Have one student give directions to others to complete a complicated task. After doing one or several of these communication activities, discuss the usefulness of having multiple perspectives.

Interviewing others. Students take a simple question such as "where is your favorite place to be and why?" and interview other students, repeating their answers back to them and then preparing a short paragraph, collage, poem, or other art form to express the other's perspective.

Take the Perspective of Others by Taking an Alternative Perspective

Ideas for Developing Skills

Level 3: Practice Procedures
Set goals, Plan steps of problem solving, Practice skills

Entering literature. Ask students to take the perspective of a character from literature and write a letter from the character to themselves (the students) or to another character from the same story on a particular topic. For a literature comparison, ask them to write the letter as if it was from one character to another character from a different story.

Perspectives in current events. Choose a few current conflicts that the students can understand and lead a discussion of why each of these conflicts exists. Try to get them to realize that conflict typically occurs when there are two different perspectives. Encourage acknowledgement of both sides of the conflict while suspending judgment of who's "right" and who's "wrong." If appropriate, proceed with a discussion of what issues to weigh and standards to use if one is going to take sides in the conflict.

Empathy in literature. The following stories provide a context for the students to practice emotional perspective-taking (guessing how another person would feel), which is a step toward developing empathy (actually feeling what another person would feel): *Cracker Jackson*, by B. Byars; *The Hundred Dresses*, by E. Ester; *The Rag Coat*, by L. Mills. Students can write letters or poetry from the perspective of the main character to express the emotions the characters might have felt.

Level 4: Integrate Knowledge and Procedures
Execute plans, Solve problems

Storytelling history. Have students take a historical or current event and construct a story of how the events unfolded from the perspective(s) of the people affected. (See *A Multicultural Approach to Education*, Sleeter & Grant, 1998, p. 139, for an example with Mexican-American immigration or *Critical Thinking Handbook*, Paul, 1987, p. 266, for a Spanish colonist/California Indians example).

Expressing a story from the community. Have students interview someone from the community and artistically tell their life story through writing or other performance media (see *A Multicultural Approach to Education*, Sleeter & Grant, 1998, p. 109 for examples).

Take the Perspective of Others by Taking an Alternative Perspective

Ideas for Developing Skills

Level 4 (continued)

Considering multiple perspectives leads to a better solution. Have students construct a survey or interview with which they can poll classmates or family members (topics could include opinions about school or community buildings, team spirit, safety, friendliness, etc.). As they tally the votes and prepare a summary of the results, ask them to list some of the reasons why people's responses to the same question might be different. If appropriate, have the students construct an action plan to address some of the concerns they learned about in their survey. This action plan should include several perspectives on the issue.

Assessment Hints

Take an Alternative Perspective

Use art or writing. Students portray an issue or conflict from more than one perspective.

Role-play. Students role-play other's perspectives in a dilemma or dialogue.

Producing a work of art/literature. Students portray another's perspective.

Individual performance. Following a cooperative or class activity targeting a particular sensitivity skill, students are assessed on their individual performance using a new example.

Take the Perspective of Others by Taking a Cultural Perspective

Arthur Golden, author of *Memoirs of a Geisha*, entranced English-speaking readers by taking them into another time as well as another culture. **Amy Tan, Pearl Buck**, and **Toni Morrison** do the same thing with other cultures. They all provide readers with a broad knowledge base of the culture and time period, including attitudes and emotions, that allows us to take the perspectives of their characters.

Ideas for Developing Skills

Level 1: Immersion in Examples and Opportunities
Attend to the big picture, Learn to recognize basic patterns

Simulation of being in a foreign culture. Use one of the intercultural simulations such as Barnga, in which students experience the frustration and helplessness of being unable to figure out a new culture. (You can either order the Barnga game from Intercultural Press or read about how to set it up in *Intercultural Sourcebook: Cross-Cultural Training Methods* by Fowler & Mumford, 1995.) In this game, the teacher distributes a pack of cards and written game rules to each group of students. Unbeknownst to them, each group receives a different set of rules and the students are told to play the game in complete silence. The first round goes well and then half the students rotate into another group and begin playing. Since their new group is following a different set of rules (which they probably won't realize), the experience simulates that of being in a new culture and not knowing how to act or communicate. It gives the whole class a common experience to relate to as the teacher brings up issues of culture, expectations, and intercultural conflict.

Cultural traditions. Identify an area of life in which students' families will differ (this will vary by community). For example: winter holiday celebrated, what the family does for July 4th, or birthday celebration traditions. Have each student interview their family elders for information about the sources of their family's traditions. Discuss in class the sources of differences (e.g., culture, historical circumstance as with lutefisk).

Take the Perspective of Others by Taking a Cultural Perspective

Ideas for Developing Skills

Level 2: Attention to Facts and Skills
Focus on detail and prototypical knowledge, Build knowledge

Culture holiday 20 questions. Play this game in pairs or as a whole class. Research a somewhat obscure cultural event or holiday and allow students to ask yes or no questions about the significance of the event. They will have to begin to let go of some of their assumptions, which is one of the first steps in perspective-taking.

Cultural/ethnic perspectives in poetry. Read poems that address a specific issue of race, ethnicity, and culture: for example, *The Palm of My Heart: Poetry by African-American Children* (Adedjouma, 1996). Poetry from other identity groups can be found on the internet and the library. Discuss the perspective the author conveys.

Local perspectives. Have students research (by interviewing local leaders, visiting local museums, etc.) and present the different understandings of a local tradition (e.g., for fishing in Minnesota, one perspective is the Native American view of fishing as subsistence as well as part of their culture, while fishing is a sport to many macroculture Americans).

Time period differences. Immerse students in daily living during another time period by: (1) visiting a live folk history museum like Fort Snelling; (2) inviting an elder from the community to discuss how life was when he or she was young; (3) watching a period drama or television show like 1900, about a family living in 19th century circumstances. Discuss how the living conditions would affect the daily activities that the students are accustomed to.

Level 3: Practice Procedures
Set goals, Plan steps of problem solving, Practice skills

Teaching our culture. Using journals or role plays, have students describe a familiar American tradition (like football or the 4th of July) to an imaginary person who knows nothing about American culture. Alternatively they could describe a piece of culture to an "alien" who knows nothing about humans.

Take the Perspective of Others by Taking a Cultural Perspective

Ideas for Developing Skills

Level 3 (continued)

Writing letters using cultural perspectives in literature. The following chapter books address issues of race, ethnicity or culture: *Remember My Name*, by S. Banks; *Escape to Freedom*, by O. Davis; *Sing Down the Moon*, by S. O'Dell; *Park's Quest*, by K. Paterson; *Taking Sides*, by G. Soto; *The Sign of the Beaver*, by E. Speare; *Let the Circle Be Unbroken*, by M. Taylor; *Mississippi Bridge*, by M. Taylor; *Roll of Thunder Hear My Cry*, by M. Taylor; *Song of the Trees*, by M. Taylor; *The Devil's Arithmetic*, by J. Yolen. Have students write letters as if they were one character speaking to another, or one of the characters writing to the students themselves.

Intercultural perspective-taking. Use critical incidents (short stories in which a cultural misunderstanding occurs) to have students discuss perspective-taking and brainstorm on how to deal with intercultural misunderstandings. Try to focus on many types of intercultural encounters (cross-age, cross-gender, cross-social class) rather than just ethnic differences. Allow students to role play (if they can handle it), switching perspectives to "try on" both sides and to allow them to practice ways of dealing with the problem. (See Appendix for some critical incidents involving culture.)

Level 4: Integrate Knowledge and Procedures
Execute plans, Solve problems

Culture perspectives in history. Have students take a historical or current event involving more than one culture and find out about the participants' views of the matter. Have students construct stories of how the events unfolded from the perspectives of each participant. (See *A Multicultural Approach to Education*, Sleeter & Grant, 1998, p. 139, for an example with Mexican-American immigration or *Critical Thinking Handbook*, Paul, 1987, p. 266, for a Spanish colonist/California Indians example.)

Expressing the story of someone from a different culture. Have students interview someone in the community from a different culture. Interview questions can include experiences in their home country, their cultural traditions, their reactions to American culture, and how they feel about their own culture. If it is not possible for every student to interview someone, the whole class can interview a visitor from another culture. The students should prepare a set of respectful questions to ask him/her, and then work individually or in small groups to artistically tell the interviewee's life story through writing or other performance media.

Assessment Hints

Take a Cultural Perspective

Use art or writing. Students portray an issue or conflict from more than one cultural perspective.

Role-play. Students role-play other cultural perspectives in a dilemma or dialogue.

Producing a work of art/ literature. Students portray another cultural perspective.

Individual performance. Following a cooperative or class activity targeting a particular sensitivity skill, students are assessed on their individual performance using a new example

Take the Perspective of Others by Taking a Justice Perspective

Jonathan Kozol is known for consciously leaving comfortable surroundings to work in impovershed, challenging environments. He has written several books that involve his first-hand experiences with social problems (e.g., segregated and unequal schools, illiteracy, and homelessness). In his books, Mr. Kozol humanizes these abstract problems by taking the perspectives of particular individuals who are directly affected by these issues as well as taking a justice-oriented perspective.

Creative and Expert Implementer Real-Life Example

Ideas for Developing Skills

Level 1: Immersion in Examples and Opportunities
Attend to the big picture, Learn to recognize basic patterns

What is fortune? Investigate different perspectives of fortune.
(1) What does my country historically think fortune is (looks like)? Read historic documents like the Declaration of Independence to find out what was in the minds of those who designed the United States.
(2) What does the media suggest that fortune is? Analyze advertisements on television and in print media for the messages they send about what is important and what a person's goals should be.
(3) What does my community believe fortune is? Interview leaders from non-government organizations, government service, politics, religion, business.

Affluenza. Investigate the notion of affluenza, the addiction to things at the expense of the rest of life. For information and websites, see http://www.diseaseworld.com/afflu.htm

What is the good life? Investigate different perspectives of the good life. Have students investigate philosophy, positive psychology, religion, and so on. Write (and illustrate?) the different perspectives on a large newsprint roll and display in the classroom or hallway.

Level 2: Attention to Facts and Skills
Focus on detail and prototypical knowledge, Build knowledge

Who is less fortunate in my community? Invite community leaders to discuss who are the needy in the community. What measures do they use to find out this information?

Take the Perspective of Others by Taking a Justice Perspective

Ideas for Developing Skills

Level 2 (continued)

What do people do to help the less fortunate? Invite community leaders to speak about what is done locally for the less fortunate. Prepare for the speakers' visits with web investigations about the poor and needy.

The problem of homelessness.
(1) Learn about homelessness in the U.S. (www.endhomelessnow.org).
(2) Learn about homelessness in your community by contacting agencies who work with the homeless, government officials who keep statistics.

Level 3: Practice Procedures
Set goals, Plan steps of problem solving, Practice skills

The problem of hunger.
(1) Learn about hunger in the U.S. and worldwide. Visit websites like Bread for the World (www.bread.org) for fact sheets, links and other materials.
(2) Investigate the incidence of hunger in your local community. Invite the director of a local food bank.
(3) Participate in World Vision's 30-hour long fast that raises money for the hungry of the world. More information:
http://www.30hourfamine.org

The problem of poverty.
Jigsaw. For information to use in a jigsaw, search on the web for "50 facts about poverty" "Myths and facts about poverty and welfare" or go to the Bread for the World website (www.bread.org).

Abstain.
Select something common to all the students that the poor do not have access to that the class agrees to abstain from for a period of time (e.g., a week). During the time and afterwards, reflect on what it was like.

Take the Perspective of Others by Taking a Justice Perspective

Ideas for Developing Skills

Level 4: Integrate Knowledge and Procedures
Execute plans, Solve problems

Carry out a project to help the homeless. Help the homeless (for 54 suggestions, see http://www.earthsystems.org/ways/). Among the suggestions are (1) Teach others about homelessness. (2) Collect toys for donations. (3) Raise money to donate. (4) Play with children at a shelter. (5) Prepare and give food. (6) Collect other needed items to donate (e.g., toiletries).

Simulation of poverty. Have older students participate in a simulation of poverty. For more information, see http://www.ext.vt.edu/news/releases/111898/poverty.html

Raise money. Kids can make a difference (http://www.kids.maine.org/hunfa.htm) outlines several ideas for raising money including holding a walk/dance/read-a-thon, a student-faculty playoff, an art show, a costume ball, a justice-quilt raffle, poetry reading, a fast, an auction. Select one of these and carry it out.

Run an information campaign. With the help of a local (volunteer) publicist or advertising executive, design a campaign to inform the public about one problem of the needy in the local community. This will require selection of a problem to highlight, discussion of possible messages, discussion of actions to recommend. The students should also give speeches, testify at local city council meetings, lobby for change.

Assessment Hints

Take a Justice Perspective

Communications. Have students write and post communications (e.g., eports, posters, public service announcements, speeches) about justice issues.

Social action. Have students take social action through petitions, demonstrations, letter writing, advocacy, campaigning.

Create a Climate
to Develop Perspective-Taking Skills

Integrate social perspective-taking into the curriculum:
- Present multiple viewpoints in the curriculum when relevant.
- Provide opportunities for student input into curriculum when possible.
- Discuss the value conflicts and moral dilemmas that arise in lessons.
- Impart multicultural information in an exciting, positive, interesting manner.

Emphasize other perspectives in curriculum and in personal action.

Emphasize responsibilities to others.

Bring up the less fortunate when you discuss the effects of actions on others.

Sample Student Self-Monitoring
Taking the Perspectives of Others

Encourage active learning by having students learn to monitor their own learning

Take an Alternative Perspective

What do I/should I focus on in this situation?

How many and which people are affected by this situation?

How are the different people affected or how could they be affected?

What are their circumstances?

How does this look to someone with their background?

Take a Cultural Perspective

What about their backgrounds will affect their perspectives in this situation?

Do I know enough about their backgrounds to understand how the situation looks to them?

If not, what are some ways I could find out more about their backgrounds and perspectives?

Take a Justice Perspective

I am able to think of the needy.

I know where to look for the less fortunate.

I am concerned about the less fortunate.

I know some things I can do to help the less fortunate.

ES-2 Taking the Perspective of Others

Ethical Sensitivity 3

Connecting to Others
(Care for others)

WHAT

Connecting to others involves expanding the sense of self-concern to include others. It also involves developing a sense of connectedness to other people/groups, both globally and locally. A person who feels a sense of connection to others is more likely to make decisions and take actions that reflect care and concern for others. Students need to learn the skills of showing and friendship so that they can connect positively to others.

WHY

In order to experience empathy or any sense of concern for others, an individual must be willing and able to perceive and interpret others as being connected to the self. When this is the case, she or he is more likely to make decisions and take actions that reflect care and concern for others, meet others' needs, and nurture relationships.

SUBSKILLS OVERVIEW

1: Relate to others
   What happens to others, happens to you
2: Show care
   Developing empathy
   Taking action respectfully
3: Be friend
   Being a friend is rewarding
   Maintaining friendships takes work

"Education fails when it neglects school as a form of community life."
-John Dewey (as quoted in Archambault, 1964, p. 431)

Web Wise

Important information for kids on relationships are at www.safeyouth.org and www.nobully.org

Connecting to Others by Relating to Them

The Buddhist philosopher, **Thich Nhat Hahn**, is a master of understanding how people are interrelated. He says that when he looks at a blank piece of paper, he feels connected to the people at the paper mill, to the logger who cut down the tree that made the paper, to the logger's parents, to the person who made the logger's breakfast, to the clouds that produced the rain that made the tree grow (from *The Heart of Understanding*, 1988). He takes this deep process of perceiving interrelatedness into his daily life so that he is able to feel compassion for all living things.

Creative and Expert Implementer Real-Life Example

Ideas for Developing Skills

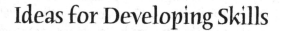

Level 1: Immersion in Examples and Opportunities
Attend to the big picture, Learn to recognize basic patterns

Interdependence activities. Students participate in activities that demonstrate interdependence, such as a ropes course or a project that requires individuals with different strengths to play different roles.

Identifying connections in community. Have the students identify relations to people in the neighborhood such as the people who live in houses and apartments nearby or the service personnel that service the neighborhood (e.g., mail carrier, police officers in the precinct, grocery store owners, business owners). Depict these graphically with lines connecting them. ⭐

Interdependence in a community. (1) Have students finish the sentence, "I'm important to this class because..." or "I'm important my family/school/community, because..." (2) Have students draw a diagram, putting themselves in the middle, of all the people they come in contact with regularly. They can add to the diagram the strangers who support their lifestyle (farmers, grocers, movie producers, candy manufacturers, etc.). Have students also draw in connections between community members (this should make a large web). ⭐

Focus on other people's positive traits. Have students practice looking for the positive traits in other people in what they read and in everyday life. In the margin is a list of positive traits to use.

Postive Traits

Accepting	Knowledgeable
Adaptable	Lively
Assertive	Loving
Bold	Mature
Brave	Modest
Calm	Observant
Carefree	Patient
Caring	Playful
Cheerful	Pleasant
Clever	Principled
Confident	Rational
Courageous	Realistic
Creative	Reasonable
Dependable	Reflective
Disciplined	Relaxed
Dutiful	Reliable
Energetic	Respectful
Fair	Responsible
Friendly	Responsive
Gentle	Self aware
Giving	Sensible
Happy	Skillful
Helpful	Sociable
Honorable	Tactful
Idealistic	Thoughtful
Imaginative	Trusting
Independent	Trustworthy
Intelligent	Understanding
Kind	

ES-3 Connecting to Others

Starred ⭐ activities within each subskill go together!

Connecting to Others by Relating to Them

Ideas for Developing Skills

Level 2: Attention to Facts and Skills
Focus on detail and prototypical knowledge, Build knowledge

Setting mutual expectations in class meeting. Set goals and rules with the students. Let them help set classroom policies on a few selected issues, including role-playing how the policies would play out in a couple different situations. Teacher can act as a facilitator with "veto power." Assess by giving each student credit for participation once the whole class successfully establishes a set of goals or rules. Have the group assess how each rule affects their interdependence.

Are we part of the problem? Have students bring in news clippings of tragic events or dismal circumstances at the local, national, and global levels. As a class reflect on how we may directly or indirectly contribute to the problem and have individual students journal on how they could make even one small change to make the situation better. To help get them started, give a few examples that exemplify creativity, leadership, or other qualities you might want to work on.

 Personal responsibilities to community: bumper stickers and ads. Have the students identify relations with and responsibilities in the neighborhood such as not littering, not making too much noise, being courteous to neighbors, not hurting anyone or their property, etc. and make bumper stickers or video/audio commercials promoting these responsibilities.

 Symbiosis in nature. Have students use a variety of resources (books, nature magazines, internet, video) to identify examples of symbiosis in nature. Discuss how these relationships are similar to and different from human interdependence.

Level 3: Practice Procedures
Set goals, Plan steps of problem solving, Practice skills

Interdependence in current events. (1) Have students survey periodicals and news shows and determine the percentage of stories that impact them in various categories: e.g., entertainment, quality of local environment, laws for behavior on the street, political expression, education, safety. (2) Select a non-local current event and discuss how it impacts the students' local communities, school, family, etc.

Interdependence among communities in current events. (1) Select a non-local current event and discuss how it affects the students' local communities, school, families, etc. (2) Select a local current event and discuss how it affects students and communities elsewhere.

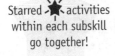 Starred activities within each subskill go together!

Connecting to Others by Relating to Them

Ideas for Developing Skills

Level 3 (continued)

Using knowledge of interdependence in decision-making. After completing some lower level work on interdependence, let students reason through hypothetical dilemmas (see Appendix) in small groups or as a whole class. If they don't bring up interdependence on their own, suggest that they re-frame the situation keeping interdependence in mind. Then ask them to reflect on whether this changes the types of options, solutions, or consequences they generate.

Groups relating to groups. Have students map out the relationships and decision making procedures of one or more of the following. (1) Investigate how civic groups work with government agencies and with the religious community to solve community problems. (2) Investigate how counties relate to townships, cities, the state and other forms of government. (3) Investigate how people at the school district/corporation work together. How do they make decisions everyone has to live with? (4) Investigate the different groups of workers at your school. How do the groups work with each other—informing each other of events, of changes, of emergencies? (5) Investigate a manufacturing plant and how the assembly line works together to produce a product.

Level 4: Integrate Knowledge and Procedures
Execute plans, Solve problems

Interdependence as a philosophical/religious worldview. Pick a couple short readings by a philosopher (like Thich Nhat Hahn) who writes short and easy to read descriptions of interdependence as part of the Buddhist worldview, and ask students to journal or discuss their reactions to this worldview. Do they agree with it? How does it conflict with American worldviews?

What if? Have students watch a film like *It's a Wonderful Life* and discuss the impact one person can have and how interdependent people are for their fates. Have students write about what would happen if they did not fulfill their responsibilities.

Interdependence in the environment. Help reinforce the school's recycling practices/policies by constructing posters that depict how humans, animals, plants, and all of nature are interconnected and how the consequences for nature affect us. See *Save Our Planet: 52 Things Kids Can Do* (Levine, 1990) for ideas on feasible nature conservation projects for the students.

Starred ★ activities within each subskill go together!

Assessment Hints

Relate to Others

Essays. Students write about personal connections valued by the student.

Planning. Students participate in a community service project that demonstrates connection and interdependence within the school or community.

Journaling. Students write about who they feel close to in the community/the world/at school and why.

Reports. Students write reports on a disadvantaged person or group of people demonstrating their connection to the student and/or the student's community.

Individual performance. Following a cooperative or class activity targeting a particular sensitivity skill, students are assessed on their individual performance using a new example.

Connect to Others by Showing Care

Mother Theresa was a master at identifying the needs of others and caring for them in a humble, respectful manner.

Ideas for Developing Skills

Level 1: Immersion in Examples and Opportunities
Attend to the big picture, Learn to recognize basic patterns

Students' Bill of Rights. In conjunction with regular class meetings, consider letting the students draft a bill of rights, stating basic expectations for the way they expect to be treated by one another. Make sure each student has a chance for input and signs the document and then post it in classroom.

Compassion in literature. While there are plenty of classic stories of compassion in the Bible and Book of Virtues, here are some chapter books that provide a shared context from which students can start to define compassion: *One-eyed Cat*, by P. Fox; *Slave Dancer*, by P. Fox; *The Rag Coat*, by L. Mills; *The Comeback Dog*, by J. Thomas.

Observations of care. Have students watch a film or video and pick out instances where someone showed care for another person, a group of people, nature, or future generations.

What is empathy? Empathy cannot be directly taught because it is impossible to "make" a student feel an emotion, but it can be modeled and discussed. Introduce the term and challenge the students to think of how empathy is different from sympathy (sympathy is feeling sorry for the person, but empathy is feeling exactly what the other person is feeling). How is perspective-taking different? (Perspective-taking involves seeing the other person's point of view, but not necessarily having any emotions about it). Ask students to think about themselves being in a tough situation and whether they would like someone else to empathize, sympathize, or take their perspective. Also talk about why humans have empathy (and maybe not other animals) and how people express it.

> First steps to finding love is to pay attention to other people's feelings. Watch how others do it. Ask for advice.

Connect to Others by Showing Care

Ideas for Developing Skills

Level 2: Attention to Facts and Skills
Focus on detail and prototypical knowledge, Build knowledge

Everyday caring. Devote a bulletin board or poster area to visually display ways of caring. Ask students to bring in news clippings, artwork, or poetry that depict caring toward people we see and interact with everyday (parents, bus drivers, teachers, siblings, etc.).

How do you show care? Have students interview community members about how they think care for others should be/can be shown in particular situations. (Keep in mind that there will be differences in how to show care to people of different ages.) Students can prepare a report or poster to share with the class.

Cultural differences in showing care. Have students find information (interviews, internet) about how care is shown to others in different cultures. Have the class make a chart comparing and/or contrasting the different ways.

Showing care with empathic responses. Empathy is the ability to listen and to express understanding of what is being expressed. It is the ability of the person to connect with the feelings of another without getting 'lost' in them. Empathic responses help establish trust and respect, encourage the speaker to keep speaking, and provide clarification of issues, statements and feelings for both the listener and the speaker. To show empathy you must demonstrate an awareness of the content of the statement made by the speaker (this is usually done with a paraphrase of the statement) and an awareness of the feelings being expressed (listener reflects feelings in a statement). For example, if the speaker says "I can't wait to see him! We have so much to talk about." The listener could say: "You really want to get together soon and catch up on things" (paraphrase) or "You're excited about seeing him" (reflection of feelings).

How to care for someone who is upset (based on example in Gibbs, Potter, & Goldstein, 1995). Have students practice the following steps (thinking outloud) for caring for someone who is upset: (1) Pay attention to the person but don't stare. What feelings do you sense? How strong are the feelings? (2) Plan what to do. Decide how to help. Should you walk over to them now, or wait until they calm down? (3) Start a conversation. Try to choose a way that is not threatening or patronizing. (4) Listen to what the person says and show empathy (see activity above on showing empathy).

ES-3 Connecting to Others

Starred activities within each subskill go together!

Connect to Others by Showing Care

Ideas for Developing Skills

Level 2 (continued)

Express appreciation (from Gibbs, Potter, & Goldstein, 1995). Have students practice the following steps. (1) Think about whether the person would like to hear that you appreciate him or her? How might the person react? (2) Plan ahead. Imagine what you will say. When and where will you say it? (3) Speak to the person in a friendly way. Examples of situations to role play: (a) Thank a teacher for something he or she has done. (b) Tell your parents or guardians that you love them. (c) Your friend has given you the cd that you wanted.

Level 3: Practice Procedures
Set goals, Plan steps of problem solving, Practice skills

Non-local volunteering. When a disaster strikes outside the community (e.g., flood), students brainstorm on how to help. Plan it and then do it. This allows students to feel connected to others who are affected by natural disasters, political turmoil, and economic hardship (i.e., even a recession in a rural area).

Local community service. Invest time and work locally so students feel connected and effective within the community. Set up times and places for the students to do community service (keeping in mind that research shows that for middle school students, community service with disadvantaged people aggravates stereotypes). Make sure to reflect on the experiences together. Assess written reflections by grading with a rubric (see Appendix for sample rubric).

Secret pal. Students are assigned a classmate or younger schoolmate to whom they give positive communication secretly for a short period of time. Discuss permissible ways to communicate positive feelings (e.g., positive notes stuck in their locker) ahead of time. Limit the time to one day or one week. Students keep track of their pal's reactions to their positive communication.

Helping across borders. Have students conduct interviews, library research, and internet research to explore how their community helps people in other countries (by attending meetings, organizing aid, etc.). Have students identify ways that they can get involved in this outreach and organize a 'task force,' if appropriate. This is a good way for different types of students to have an opportunity to take a leadership role (especially those who don't typically take school leadership positions).

Starred activities within each subskill go together!

Connect to Others by Showing Care

Ideas for Developing Skills

Level 3 (continued)

Practice showing care in culturally different ways. After gathering cultural information (Level 2), have students practice these different ways of showing care. If possible, ask a member of that culture to assess how well they are doing.

Showing care by attending. (1) Have students practice the following attending skills while having a conversation with a partner: Appropriate eye contact (no staring or constant looking away); Comfortable relaxed posture focused on your partner; Careful listening (e.g., let the partner finish his/her sentences, note the partner's nonverbal expressions like tone of voice, body language); Gently question to help your partner express his/her ideas and feelings; Show warmth and positive regard; Use a soft tone of voice; Use nods of the head and verbalizations to show you are listening (e.g., mm-hmmm, I see); Be genuine and spontaneous; Be alert and sensitive; Be non-judgmental in your attitude and behavior; Match your partner's behaviors and feelings (don't be smiling when the partner is sad or angry); Avoid unhelpful behaviors (e.g., interrupting, yawning, frowning, showing boredom, slouching). (2) Have students practice for a period of time outside of class and then test them with a role play in class. (3) Have students practice doing these things with different age groups (e.g., young children, older adults, etc.).

Showing care in a particular role. Have students gather information and examples about showing empathy and attending in a particular role, for example, older sibling to a younger sibling, mentor to mentee, older student to younger student, student to adult stranger, student to teacher, student to adult acquaintance, child to parent, parent to child, student to family, student to classmates, student to school, and so on. Discuss what changes and does not change across these different role situations.

Level 4: Integrate Knowledge and Procedures
Execute plans, Solve problems

Guided social action. Students take the steps in noticing a need in the community, communicating with relevant people/agencies, building an action plan, and implementing the plan. Example: students initiate and implement a plan to make the community aware of pollution in a local river, including radio and newspaper publicity, gathering facts, and organizing a community forum to discuss possible solutions (see *Kid's Guide to Social Action*, Lewis et al, 1998, for more ideas). The important element is student ownership.

Mock United Nations or FEMA (Federal Emergency Management Agency) activity. Set up a small FEMA to support the needs of other students. Students organize different groups representing the needs of various people and work to serve as many as possible of those needs.

Starred activities within each subskill go together!

Connect to Others by Showing Care

Ideas for Developing Skills

Level 4 (continued)

Finding common ground. Ask students to creatively help two different groups within the community find common ground on some issue of conflict. This could be done individually, in small groups, or as a class. Break down the steps into: identify the perspective of each side, identify the goals of each side, find common perspectives and establish common goals.

Caring in local settings. Have students keep a journal about how they show care in a community setting (volunteering). Ask a community member to assess how well they showed care there.

Start a compassion club. Use the information and ideas gathered about showing compassion and empathy to develop a charter for a club dedicated to showing compassion.

Compassion skills initiative. Have students develop and carry out a plan for teaching others about being more compassionate.

Assessment Hints

Show care

Essays. Students write about times when they have received care or shown care.

Planning. Students participate in a community service project that shows care to other people, the environment, to the community, etc.

Journaling. Students write about how they show care for the community/world/school and why.

Individual performance. Following a cooperative or class activity targeting a particular sensitivity skill, students are assessed on their individual performance using a new example.

Connect to Others by Being a Friend

Many people think of marriage as the ultimate friendship. Think of someone you know who has been happily married for a very long time and how much work they have put into the friendship in order to sustain and nurture both people in the marriage. An example of a well-known marriage was that of famous actor/comedian **Bob Hope** and singer **Dolores Reade**, who were married for 67 years.

Creative and Expert Implementer Real-Life Example

Ideas for Developing Skills

Level 1: Immersion in Examples and Opportunities
Attend to the big picture, Learn to recognize basic patterns

Getting to know each other: Introductions. Set up a 10-minute partner activity for students to interview each other (see chart in Lickona's *Educating For Character*, 1992, p.92). Each person introduces their partner to the rest of the class with a small report. Assess the quality of interviews (completeness and following directions) using a rubric like the sample in the Appendix.

Getting to know each other: Partners. Two people discuss ways they are alike, ways they are different, their particular likes and dislikes (e.g., foods, movies, favorite subject), their families.

Getting to know each other: People Hunt. Give students a list of 20 items and tell them to fill in people's names for as many items as possible. For example: likes to play basketball, likes to ride horses, likes pizza.

Getting to know each other: Snapshots. Display photos of students on bulletin board, perhaps with collage "self-portraits" (display of any pictures, drawings, words, objects, etc. that the student feels represents him/herself).

Stories of friendship. Students read stories about friendship and then discuss how the characters acted as friends and how they created and/or maintained their friendship. The discussion could involve talking about how the characters thought about friendship and whether the characters acted as true friends. Students could also write a revision of the story where the characters are better friends than in the original story. In pairs or in a group, students could also act out the revision.

Examples of friendship. Show examples of how good friends treat each other (e.g., excerpts from television shows like WB's *Smallville*, or examples from literature).

ES-3 Connecting to Others

Connect to Others by Being a Friend

Ideas for Developing Skills

Level 2: Attention to Facts and Skills
Focus on detail and prototypical knowledge, Build knowledge

Relationship journal. Have students keep a journal for several weeks in which they discuss their relationships. Are some of the relationships friend relationships? What is different about a friend relationship? If a student does not have a friend, have them imagine a friend and write about what the relationship would be like.

Contrast friendship with other relationships. Have students interview community members about their friendships in contrast to other relationships. They can write essays about what they learned. Assess by grading essays with a rubric.

Benefits of friendship. Ask students to reflect on the importance of friendship (for being able to solve practical problems, for being able to solve personal problems, for enjoying common hobbies, for being happy, for staying healthy, etc). This could be culminated in a collage or poster activity to depict the different kinds of benefits.

Getting a friend by being a friend. Everyone needs to have a friend who listens to you, accepts you, and supports you. Friel and Friel (*The 7 Best Things Smart Teens Do*, 2000) suggest that teens make a diagram of their social world, of the key relationships they have, placing themselves at the center and putting the others at a distance that represents how important the relationship is. The students should draw circles around each name, the size of which depends on how strong the relationship is. All familiar relatives should be included. Then students should ask themselves, if they were in trouble (name some specific ways representative of the school), to whom would they turn for help? This should change the diagram, eliminating some people and making others (usually relatives) more important. If students have very few supports, this honest look can help them realize it and make some changes. Making friends is a skill they can work on.

Level 3: Practice Procedures
Set goals, Plan steps of problem solving, Practice skills

Study buddy. Assign study buddies, or learning partners, for the year. Let them know that they are responsible for helping each other, especially when one of them is struggling (see p. 72 in Ladson-Billings's *The Dreamkeepers*, 1997, for example). Regularly discuss how things are going, what conflicts have arisen and how they are resolved.

Characteristics of people who are liked as friends

(1) Fun to be with

(2) Treat others like equals

(3) Responsive to needs and emotions of others

(4) Willing to trust others with information about self

(5) Able to express caring

(6) Resolve conflict and compromise

(7) Able to forgive

(8) See friendship as part of a context of relationships

Starred ★ activities within each subskill go together!

Connect to Others by Being a Friend

Ideas for Developing Skills

Level 3 (continued)

Reflecting on friendships in different domains. Students write about friendship, comparing and contrasting how it looks in the neighborhood, at church, in sport, in the family. How do you show caring in these different places?

Pen Pal. Students create and maintain a pen pal relationship with someone different from them. After a set period of time, everyone reflects on the experience.

Friends of different ages. Ask students to reflect on friends who are different ages (young child, elderly adult). They can journal on their experiences and how the friendships differ.

Having a mentor. Students interact regularly with older kids in the community who are taking social action and are involved in their communities.

Level 4: Integrate Knowledge and Procedures
Execute plans, Solve problems

Cross-cultural connecting. Ask the students to role-play or write a dialogue about how each could make a connection with a new neighbor from a different country. They should display awareness of cultural and perspective differences.

Being a mentor. Set up cross-age mentoring projects in which students pair or team up with younger students to complete projects for the community or even to help the younger students with their homework.

Assessment Hints

Be a friend

Essays. Students write about personal friendships valued by the student.

Journaling. Students write about who they feel close to in the community/world/school and why.

Write letters. Students write letters to a pen pal and establish connections (interdependence) and similarities.

Starred activities within each subskill go together!

ES-3 Connecting to Others

Create a Climate
to Develop Connecting to Others

Discuss responsibility to others and to the world

Teach about ecological interdependence by using inductive discipline, discussing effects of prosocial acts on others.

Model caring by being a responsive teacher

Communicate with each student personally each day.
Figure out how to make each student feel welcomed and supported.
Coach a student when he or she is having difficulty with schoolwork.
Try to find out what will help each student succeed in class.
>*By asking parents
>*By asking the students themselves
>*By consulting the relevant experts, if appropriate

Provide safety/security

Encourage the students to avoid negative attitudes.
Expect students to treat each other with respect.
Encourage the students to not develop an "us against them" mentality.
Provide opportunities for appropriate and safe expressions of feelings.
Encourage a sense of healty self-respect.
Have high standards for prosocial behavior.

Provide psychological support

Be aware of students' personal lives.
Provide opportunities for developing self-awareness.
Provide opportunities for developing self-direction.
Provide opportunities for developing self-control.
Help the students learn how to get along with each other.
Provide opportunities for respectful discussion of different viewpoints.
Provide opportunities for students to meet needs normally taken care of outside the classroom (e.g., breakfast, encouragement).

Be a model

Model helping, sharing, comforting others clearly and frequently.
Model and encourage positive regard for others (including giving others the benefit of the doubt).

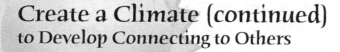

Create a Climate (continued)
to Develop Connecting to Others

Encourage friendship
Encourage friendships among the children.
Discuss the responsibilities of friendship.
Set up a class to class friendship with a distant class in which the classes communicate regularly about their activities.

Develop student connections. At the beginning of the year, help students get to know one another using one of the following techniques (from Lickona, *Educating for Character*, 1992):

<u>Partners</u>: Two people discuss ways that they are alike, ways they are different, their particular likes and dislikes (e.g., foods, movies, favorite subject), their families.

<u>People hunt</u>: Give students a list of 20 items and tell them to fill in people's names for as many items as possible. For example, "likes to play basketball," "likes to ride horses," "likes pizza."

<u>Snapshots</u> of students on bulletin board.

<u>Class directory</u>: This can be created by students interviewing each other and then writing a biographical sketch of the person interviewed to be placed in the directory.

<u>Seat lottery</u>: Rearrange seat assignments periodically by having the students select their seats via lottery system.

Sample Student Self-Monitoring
Connecting to Others

Encourage active learning by having students learn to monitor their own learning

Relate to Others

I'm important to this class because...

I'm important to my family/school/community because....

How do problems in other parts of the world affect my family?

Why is it important to think about how people are connected?

I avoid criticizing others.

I don't do things to impress others.

I learn from my mistakes.

I don't expect perfection in myself or others.

I focus on the positive things in others.

I don't think I am more important than other people.

Show Care

I am concerned about the welfare of my friends and family.

I show love to a sad friend or family member.

I am nice only to those people who are nice to me. (NOT)

I expect something in return when I help. (NOT)

I resist the temptation to be cruel to someone else.

I tease and play tricks on people I don't like. (NOT)

I hurt animals. (NOT)

I brag when I help others. (NOT)

I try to think of and do things that make others happy.

Be a friend

I know how to show friendliness in different situations.

I know how to be polite in different situations.

I thank others for helping me or complimenting me.

Responding to Diversity
(Getting along with differences)

WHAT

Working with interpersonal and group differences involves understanding how cultural groups differ and how differences can lead to conflicts and misunderstandings. It is important to understand culture in its broadest sense, as any system of shared values, behaviors and expectations. This definition allows us to include "business culture," "school culture," "soccer culture," etc. Students should develop skills for multicultural living which include the ability to shift from using one culture code to using another.

WHY

No classroom, family, community, or work environment consists of homogeneous people so it is crucial to know how to interact with different opinions, perspectives, values, and cultures in order to accomplish group tasks, make decisions, resolve conflicts, and build leadership.

ES-4 Responding to Diversity

Web Wise
Anti-Defamation League: http://www.adl.org/awod/awod_institute.html
Center for Diversity Education: http://www.diversityed.org

Ethical Sensitivity 4

Responding to Diversity

SUBSKILLS OVERVIEW

1: Work with group and individual differences
Awareness of diversity

Appreciation of effects of diversity on problem solving and communication

Gaining knowledge of other cultures

Practicing communication and problem solving in diverse context

2: Perceive diversity

3: Become multicultural
Awareness of multiple groups that one belongs to

Appreciation of benefits of cultural flexibility

Gaining knowledge of cultures connected to self

Practicing multicultural skills— being flexible in following new sets of rules

---

Building an atmosphere for acceptance includes:
(Combs, 1962)

- Encourage self revelation instead of self defense.
- Promote a sense of belonging.
- Promote the attitude that difference is good and desirable.
- Promote trust in self.
- Emphasize the ongoing character of learning.
- Create a hopeful atmosphere.

Responding to Diversity by Working with Group and Individual Differences

Anwar Sadat, Egyptian political leader, initiated a new momentum for peace that would eventually culminate in the 1978 Camp David Accords and a final peace treaty with Israel in 1979. For his efforts, Sadat won the Nobel Prize for Peace in 1975.

Creative and Expert Implementer Real-Life Example

Ideas for Developing Skills

Level 1: Immersion in Examples and Opportunities
Attend to the big picture, Learn to recognize basic patterns

Birth stories. Ease into discussion of difference with "safe" topics like birth stories (how and where they were born) and then expand to other topics of diversity from there.

Learning about another group's experiences. This is an approach to multicultural education that pays attention to a single group (try to think beyond the obvious groups based on ethnicity, gender, etc.). For example, spend a few lessons gathering facts and constructing the perspectives of child laborers in early Industrial America (see *A Multicultural Approach to Education*, Sleeter & Grant, 1998, for more ideas). Assess with content knowledge test.

Diversity in ways to beat a cold. Have students find out the ways their parents, grandparents, or local elders deal with a cold as a way to talk about diversity between and among identity groups. Assess a written or oral report using rubrics.

Diversity in basic foods. Have students identify the basic foods of the world (what is the staple of most meals in different countries, e.g., rice, bread, tortillas, pasta) using a world map. Then students identify what food their parents had growing up at most meals (usually one of the aforementioned staples). Families are eating more multiculturally as fast food diversifies (not only sandwiches but Mexican and Asian foods as well) and so discuss how this has affected their parents (and hence their children's) diets. Assess their construction of graphs of their findings.

Read a story about appreciating differences: Freak the mighty. Read the chapter book, *Freak the Mighty*, by R. Philbrick (1993) and discuss the role of differences in the story, and how the characters came to appreciate their differences.

Differences and similarities. Select a set of cultures or a set of groups with different backgrounds. Have students compare the cultures/groups to each other and how they are like or unlike the student.

Responding to Diversity by Working with Group and Individual Differences

Ideas for Developing Skills

Level 2: Attention to Facts and Skills
Focus on detail and prototypical knowledge, Build knowledge

How culture affects reactions. After learning about the values and social expectations for a particular culture or group, give the students a hypothetical situation and ask them to think about how culture might affect how someone would react.

Values in groups in our school. Using the groups "soccer team" and "band" (or similar school groups), list which skills and talents are valued in each group and then make a chart with the columns "same" and "different" to visually depict which values the groups share and which values are unique to the group.

Using a semantic map to see how culture works. Have small groups research a country or group (e.g., China) and write descriptive words or short phrases in big lettering on note cards. Collect their descriptors and attach them to the board, organizing them according to categories like work activities, leisure activities, physical descriptions, attitudes, etc. Draw lines connecting related concepts to create a semantic map. Semantic maps can help students visualize many kinds of abstract relationships, in this case, how cultures or identity groups work and hold together.

Working together in our local community. Invite a local politician or community organizer and ask them to tell stories about how they work with group and interpersonal differences.

Balancing unity and diversity in the community.
(1) Discuss what diversity is. (a) Find definitions in dictionaries, on the web, from conservative and liberal and other viewpoints. Sort out the characteristics into pros and cons. (b) Interview community leaders to find out what they think diversity means for the community.
(2) Discuss what unity means. (a) Find definitions in dictionaries, on the web, from conservative and liberal and other viewpoints. Sort out the characteristics into pros and cons. (b) Interview community leaders to find out what they think unity means for the community.
(3) Because both unity and diversity are necessary in a pluralistic democracy, discuss how we can have both unity and diversity. (a) Why is unity important? As citizens, we all have responsibilities to one another, to supporting our democratic institutions, to working for change when structures aren't working. Supporting unity means emphasizing the characteristics we share with others in the community. (b) Why is diversity important? We also are respectful of differences and want to encourage individuals to nurture their uniqueness that ultimately contributes to increased well-being of the community. Supporting diversity means nurturing the uniqueness that individuals and small groups bring to the larger community.

Responding to Diversity by Working with Group and Individual Differences

Ideas for Developing Skills

Level 3: Practice Procedures
Set goals, Plan steps of problem solving, Practice skills

Comparing cultural artifacts. Have students compare cultures using folktales or other cultural artifacts by organizing a chart to do cultural comparisons. With stories, for example, categories could be title, setting, characters, problem, magic, events, ending.

Comparing the way families work together. Within stories or culture studies, have students look for ways that families work together for a specific goal (e.g., preparing and eating a meal together; see *Multicultural Literacy*, Diamond & Moore, 1995, p. 219, for examples). Ask "Why?" and "How?" questions to compare the ways families from different identity groups work together.

Classroom Group Diversity. Have students identify different strengths among the students in the classroom that are relevant to completing a particular project (like being organized, being able to draw, having good speaking skills, etc.). Then construct work groups consisting of people with different strengths. During the work period and afterwards, have the groups reflect on how the differences affect their cooperative effort and how they might improve or change the way they would work together next time.

Working together in our school(s). Invite the principal or superintendent and ask them to discuss how they work with group and interpersonal differences. Assess written or oral report using rubrics.

The changing community. Students interview and conduct research on the evolution of the community in terms of diversity (a good film to use as a stimulant in MN is *Minnesota Pride, Minnesota Prejudice* by Twin Cities Eyewitness News KSTP which gives a history of immigration in MN). What groups came when? How did people learn to get along? What kind of diversity do we have now? Assess written or oral report using rubrics.

Partner in diversity. Have students partner with a student with a different background (different age, different gender, different neighborhood, from a different city/state, different family size, etc.). Design an interview that will allow them to teach each other about their different perspectives in particular areas (may be chosen by teacher: e.g., food preferences, family responsibilities, after school activities, goals in life, recreational activities, clothing, communication and self-expression). Each writes a report on what is learned.

Emphasizing what unites us. (a) Have students discuss what unites them as a class, what unites them with the rest of the school, with the community, with the city, the state, the nation, the globe. (b) Ask students to make a representation of the unity they describe (e.g., drawing, sculpture, semantic web). (c) Have students brainstorm about the ways that people show unity. Have them look for demonstration of these ways over a week's time and report on the findings.

Responding to Diversity by Working with Group and Individual Differences

Ideas for Developing Skills

Level 4: Integrate Knowledge and Procedures
Execute plans, Solve problems

Multiple perspectives in history. Have students read and analyze a historical speech or document to reconstruct the perspectives of the various identity groups involved in a historical issue (see *Multicultural Literacy*, Diamond & Moore, 1995, p. 225, for an example using a speech by Chief Seattle during territory disputes).

Looking ahead. Design a writing activity or small group discussion to involve students in making predictions about which identity groups might contribute or interact in various ways. For example, pick a few developing countries, have students research them, and then brainstorm on what resources and skills those communities possess that could contribute to the rest of the world. Students can also reflect on how they will be affected at the individual level, community level, and national level (see *Breaking the Ice*, Kabagarama, 1997, p. 13 for sample questions).

Intercultural dilemmas. Provide students with intercultural dilemmas (see Appendix) and ask them to think of possible reasons for the situation that are related to group or interpersonal differences.

Local community organizing. Ask students to research some local community organizations like charities, beautification committees, etc. Have the students observe and/or participate in the workings of one such group and then analyze how well the organization works with the value and perspective differences of their members and of their "clients" (which differences they work well with, which ones not so well). They can then write a report making respectful recommendations on what the organization could do to improve its human relations.

Mentoring for diversity. Have students mentor a younger student about learning to be multicultural. Ask them to make posters, skits, stories, or mini-lessons teaching their mentees how to function in multiple groups and still stay true to their own identity and values.

Personal emphasis on unity. Have students use the list from "Emphasizing what unites us-(c)" and demonstrate unity over a week's time through actions they have identified.

Take action for unity. Hold a teach-in or unity rally in your school or community.

Assessment Hints

Working with group and individual differences

Knowledge test (on specific culture or identity group). Students demonstrate in-depth knowledge about the way an identity group functions (beyond surface details like, "what do they eat in this culture?").

Creative project. Students write about how they will be affected by various cultures or sub-cultures.

Chart. Use graphic display methods to describe similarities and differences between and among groups that the student learns about.

Individual performance. Following a cooperative or class activity targeting a particular sensitivity skill, students are assessed on their individual performance using a new example.

Responding to Diversity by Perceiving Diversity

Creative and Expert Implementer
Real-Life Example

Edward T. Hall grew up in New Mexico, led an African American regiment in the war, and worked with Hopi and Navaho Indians. His books about intercultural communication are classics that served to found the field of intercultural communications.

Ideas for Developing Skills

On pages 101-102, we list the dimensions upon which cultures differ. Below we describe the types of level activities you might do with each of the sixteen dimensions.

Level 1: Immersion in Examples and Opportunities
Attend to the big picture, Learn to recognize basic patterns

Interviewing elders. Students interview community members about one (or more) of the questions. They take notes, write up a report. Students compile the information they gather.

Community differences. Students investigate differences in perceptions among local community members for one of the questions and then illustrate their findings.

Level 2: Attention to Facts and Skills
Focus on detail and prototypical knowledge, Build knowledge

Historical perspectives. Students investigate the history of one of the questions. What are historical views of this question? Students write a report or an essay.

Cross-domain perspectives. What are domain orientations to this question (e.g., philosophy, religion, psychology, popular culture, media)? Students write a report or an essay.

A domain question. Students focus on a domain question (e.g., social studies: political participation) and how the different cultural perspectives might affect a person's perceptions.

Responding to Diversity by Perceiving Diversity

Ideas for Developing Skills

Level 3: Practice Procedures
Set goals, Plan steps of problem solving, Practice skills

Behavior in everyday life. Students investigate the interrelationships among the questions in a particular culture—how do these views affect a person's behavior in everyday life?

Effects on work in a domain. Students investigate the implications of one or more questions on a particular domain (for example in science: what should be humans relation to nature? How would a believer in the sacredness of life act differently as a scientist from one who believes that nature should be subdued?).

Effects on society. Students write about the implications of diverse perspectives on the running of the society.

Personal assessment. Have students think about how they appear to others. List personality traits that are compatible with tolerance (e.g., compassion, curiosity, openness). List those that seem incompatible with tolerance (e.g., jealousy, bossiness, perfectionism). Have students set a goal for nurturing their more tolerant traits (from tolerance.org).

Diversity profiles. Have students create a "diversity profile" of their friends, co-workers and acquaintances (from tolerance.org).

Level 4: Integrate Knowledge and Procedures
Execute plans, Solve problems

Understanding my heritage. Students describe in detail (essay) the perspective on these questions of their cultural background.

Analyzing an intercultural encounter. Students demonstrate their knowledge by describing the values that underlie a particular intercultural encounter (from a book, film, or real life).

Assessment Hints

Perceive diversity

Role play. Have students role play people from different cultural backgrounds.

Reflective activities. Have students complete reflective activities such as essays or keeping a report diary on intercultural experiences.

Creative works. Have students create poems, songs, music, plays, or visual art that represent different perspectives of a dimension.

Responding to Diversity
by Perceiving Diversity
Ideas for Developing Skills

Dimensions of Cultural Difference
(to accompany the activities described on pp. 99-100)

1. What is time?
Time can be viewed as something within a person, as something outside a person (the clock is running). Clock hours as the construct of time, external to the self, is a historically-recent phenomenon. Cultures that have historically not had clocks use an internal clock or a social clock. Time can also be viewed as cyclical or seasonal, as progressing towards something.

2. What should human relationships be like?
Some cultures emphasize short-term, coincidental relationships (e.g., you are friends with your co-workers as you move from job to job) whereas other cultures emphasize deep, long-term, and demanding relationships.

3. How should people interact with each other?
Some cultures are very emotive where people yell at each other, argue, and are very connected emotionally. Other cultures prefer a polite, detached engagement with others. Some cultures emphasize competition, others cooperation.

4. How should males and females act differently?
How do you act if you are male vs. female? What domains are you expected to know? Some cultures have rigid roles for males and females (e.g., many Arab countries); other cultures allow more freedom for the individual preferences. How do you relate to the same sex? How do you relate to the opposite sex? Some cultures allow physical affection between persons of the same sex in public but not opposite sex couples, even if they are married.

5. What is better: youth or age?
Some cultures value the elders over youth because they carry the wisdom of experience and time. Other cultures value youth because of the emphasis on good looks and attractiveness. Who deserves automatic respect generally? Older people, males, authority figures, people who demonstrate skills, celebrities, people who are persuasive?

6. What is better: dependence or independence?
Some cultures emphasize loyalty to and dependence on a group (often called "collectivist" cultures) while other cultures emphasize self-reliance and independence, even from family (often called individualist cultures).

7. Is the culture high context or low context?
In some cultures there are many social rules that you must learn in order to behave properly in particular situations. You learn to 'read' a situation for the cues telling you how to behave. In other cultures, like the U.S. mainstream culture, there are fewer rules overall and you have to talk to others in the circumstances to learn how to behave (e.g., you often can't tell what work a person does by how they are dressed or where they are seated at the table).

8. What should be humans' relation to nature?
Cultures differ in their views of the natural world and its purpose. Some cultures treat nature as a partner throughout life, others treat nature as a subordinate, to be subdued and used, while others treat nature as a superior force to be feared. The destruction of animal and plant life without due respect is sacrilegious for long-standing nature religions.

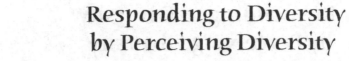

Responding to Diversity
by Perceiving Diversity
Ideas for Developing Skills

Dimensions of Cultural Difference
(to accompany the activities described on pp. 99-100)

9. What is the nature of humanity?
Are humans good, a mixture of good and evil, or basically evil? Cultures vary on their perspectives. Some say that humans are basically good and that the spirit must be allowed the freedom to grow and develop (e.g., Native American traditions). Others say that humans are basically bad, with impulses that must be controlled (e.g., Puritans, fundamentalist religions). Others say that humans are good and bad and that discipline will foster the good and control the bad (e.g., Confucius).

10. How should people spend their time?
Some cultures emphasize being—communicating with and helping others right now. Other cultures emphasize hard work, including on self improvement. Some cultures emphasize working to accomplish and change things while other cultures are fatalistic or accepting of circumstances. Cultures vary in their definitions of what is work, what is efficiency, whether or not change is good, what progress looks like.

11. What should people do in their lives?
Some cultures emphasize living a pure, respectful life in harmony with God or the spirits. Other cultures emphasize getting ahead materially, earning a good living, and having material comforts.

12. What should our relation be to material things?
Some cultures view material possessions as signs of prosperity and even personal goodness (e.g., "The person who dies with the most toys wins"). Other cultures view material possessions as ephemeral gifts that should be shared with others.

13. What is the source of truth? What is good? What is bad? What is true? What is false?
Cultures differ on what is perceived to be the source of highest truth, on what is by nature good or bad, on what is by nature right or wrong, on what is by nature true or false, on what is by nature positive or negative. Religious perspectives determine what is good or bad according to what is decreed by the religious teachings. A secularist perspective might say that what is good or bad for one's body and psyche is determined by research studies on physical and mental health or that what is right is based on basic human rights as outlined in the Declaration of Independence.

14. What forms your self-concept?
People from different cultures vary in what makes them feel worthwhile. Some feel best when they accomplish something. Some feel best when they have helped a family member or friend, or when their relationships are harmonious.

15. What is the proper attitude towards the body?
Cultures vary in attitudes towards the body such as which parts are private, which can be seen by family, which can be seen by strangers, which can be touched by others, which are sacred, which are a source of shame, and which are a source of pride.

16. What is personal?
Cultures vary on what areas of life are personal and what others can know or inquire about. In the U.S., for example, it is impolite to ask someone how much money they make. In other cultures, this is not a rude question.

Responding to Diversity by Becoming Multicultural

A rock musician (e.g., **Sting**) can recognize his or her multicultural self by acknowledging and celebrating the many cultures that built rock music: African and Afro-Caribbean rhythms, western European instruments like the guitar and piano, American jazz instrumentations, African-American gospel, fiddling traditions of the British Isles, etc.

Creative and Expert Implementer Real-Life Example

Ideas for Developing Skills

Level 1: Immersion in Examples and Opportunities
Attend to the big picture, Learn to recognize basic patterns

Identifying groups we belong to. Explore multiple groups that people belong to: formal and informal (scouting vs. kids in the neighborhood), by choice and by assignment (softball team vs. being a teenager), permanent and temporary (ethnic group vs. club). Have students interview a community member to find out what groups he or she participates in. Assess a written or oral report using rubrics.

Multiple group memberships and values. Have students interview a parent to find out what groups he or she participates in, what values his or her groups have, what is required for membership. Values can be determined by what activities and behaviors are important. Assess a written or oral report using rubrics.

Level 2: Attention to Facts and Skills
Focus on detail and prototypical knowledge, Build knowledge

Group values affect choices. Have students examine the values of an identity group and what choices are limited or offered as a result. For example, if you are black, you may be expected to avoid "acting white." If you are a boy, you may be expected to not "act like a girl." Discuss how stereotyping blackness or boy-ness limits individuals.

Comparing the values of two familiar groups. Prepare a list of identity groups including formal and informal (scouting vs. kids in the neighborhood), voluntary and involuntary (softball team vs. being a teenager), permanent and temporary (ethnic group vs. club). Ask students to pick two groups they are members of and list which skills and talents are valued in each group. Perhaps focus on which types of behaviors are expected. Then make a chart with the columns "same" and "different" to visually depict which values the groups share and which values are unique to the group. Ask them to identify at least one value that is shared by both groups, and one value that is unique to each group.

Starred 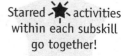 activities within each subskill go together!

Responding to Diversity by Becoming Multicultural

Ideas for Developing Skills

Level 3: Practice Procedures
Set goals, Plan steps of problem solving, Practice skills

 Exploring identity messages from different people. Have students artfully represent the messages they have received growing up from a mother, father, extended family, school, community, friends. For example, divide a sheet into several sectors, labeling them "what my parents would like me to be," "what my grandparents would like me to be," "what my friends would like me to be," etc. and illustrate those using magazine cutouts, hand-drawn art, computer-generated art, poetry, etc. Similar projects can have students reflect on "if my parents/grandparents/friends were granted one wish," or other topics that relate to values and ideals within groups.

Our language is multicultural. Have students reflect on how our language and communication reflects our multicultural background. Take a paragraph from a teen magazine and find all the words that have roots in other cultures (including American subcultures, like internet/email jargon). Ask students to research the roots of some common phrases and slang. Discuss how language "travels" and take a look at a Pidgin language like that of Hawaii, which represents a blend of the cultures that were brought by immigrants (Portuguese, Chinese, Japanese, Filipino, etc.).

Comparing the ideals of less familiar groups. Have students construct and compare lists of "what is good" or "what is ideal" to their own identity group and another comparison group (children their age from another culture, people of a different age, people trying to survive in difficult circumstances, etc.). Alternatively, use Venn diagrams to show overlap and differences.

Which self when? Have students consider the various settings they shift between and have them write about how they behave in each setting (school vs. church vs. soccer practice). Then compare and contrast "selves" across settings, noting what remains constant and what changes with context.

Level 4: Integrate Knowledge and Procedures
Execute plans, Solve problems

 How group membership affects problem solving. Help students understand that identity group membership affects the way people perceive things and solve problems. Have them examine the values of an identity group and, for a particular situation, what choices are limited or offered as a result of the values. Discuss the importance of personal and group values and how to approach dealing with clashes.

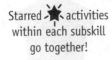 Starred activities within each subskill go together!

Responding to Diversity by Becoming Multicultural

Ideas for Developing Skills

Level 4 (continued)

Loyalty dilemmas. Give students a challenging dilemma about loyalty and discuss different ways in which the dilemma could be resolved (including the issue of when and where it is appropriate to display loyalty). These can also be dilemmas that produce conflicting loyalties (e.g., between family and community; friends and family). Students then create an implementation plan and role-play the actual implementation in small groups.

Noticing how behavior standards change across contexts. Have students keep a journal on how their behavior changes according to context. Suggest a few contexts for them to particularly notice (home with family, home alone, home with friends, shopping with friends, out with family, playing sports, in particular classrooms, on bus).

Assessment Hints

Become multicultural

Creative project. Students write about or describe their membership in multiple groups.

Chart. Use graphic display methods to describe similarities and differences between and among groups that the student belongs to or identifies with.

Individual performance. Following a cooperative or class activity targeting a particular sensitivity skill, students are assessed on their individual performance using a new example.

Create a Climate
to Develop Skills in Responding to Diversity

Lickona believes that an ethical community in the classroom requires three things (*Educating for Character*, 1991, p. 91):

1. Students know each other.
2. Students respect, affirm, and care about each other.
3. Students feel membership in, and responsibility to, the group.

Promote attention to roles

- Make it explicit what your responsibilities are and what the students' responsibilities are.
- Make explicit your expectations for student behavior.
- *Discuss the importance of being loyal to the class community and school community.*

Capitalize on student differences

Be aware of the diversity in the classroom (culture/ethnicity, socioeconomic status, family configuration, family values, ability/disability, and so on) and capitalize on it.

- Use the diversity in the classroom to help everyone learn.
- Use the diversity in the classroom to help everyone get along with each other.
- Help the students appreciate human differences.
- Help students understand and appreciate others' points of view.
- Teach about the customs and approaches of different world cultures.
- Teach about the perspectives of cultural, political, and historical experiences in different cultures.
- Teach about the diversity of cultures within the USA.

Sample Student Self-Monitoring
Responding to Diversity

Encourage active learning by having students learn to monitor their own learning

Working with group and individual differences

Are there other groups or connections that aren't obvious right now?

Should a person always try to go along with what the group wants?

Should we spend time with people who are similar to or different from ourselves?

Are my friends just like me or different from me? Is that good or bad or both or neither?

Perceive diversity

I keep in mind that other people I meet may have different perceptions.

I can describe my cultural perspectives.

I can point out an example of behavior related to each of the dimensions.

Become multicultural

What groups do I belong to?

What groups do this person and I both belong to?

What are some good things about being part of a group?

What are some bad things about being part of a group?

"Open-classroom climate generally is related to higher political efficacy and trust, and lower political cynicism and alienation—to more democratic attitudes."

(Ehman, 1980, p. 110)

Ethical Sensitivity 5

Controlling Social Bias
(Control prejudice)

WHAT

Controlling social bias involves understanding, identifying, and actively countering bias. It also means fostering the opposite of prejudice, tolerance. It is important to reflect on the nature of bias and how it comes about before attempting to control social bias. Bias is a part of human nature because we all naturally prefer familiar things and familiar ways of thinking. It takes conscious effort to rethink our personal habits of acting and speaking, but it can promote a more respectful, fair society.

WHY

Bias is a part of human nature because we all naturally prefer familiar things and familiar ways of thinking. It takes conscious effort to rethink our personal habits of acting and speaking, but it can promote a more respectful, fair society. These skills are required for both large and small scale social reform.

SUBSKILLS OVERVIEW

1: Diagnose bias
Learning about human information-processing systems and how bias works

Experiencing effects of bias in simulations, etc.

Identifying bias in language, text, actions, physical habits, institutions

2: Overcome bias

3: Nurture tolerance
Taking small steps in everyday personal life

Initiating social action/reform to prevent bias

Climate characteristics necessary for self-discovery
(Combs, 1962)

- Respect for uniqueness of each individual
- Classroom as microcosm of society
- Open communication
- People rather than things are important

Web Wise
www.tolerance.org
http://www.unesco.org/tolerance/global.htm

Controlling Social Bias by Diagnosing It

Many of the great social commentators and social activists of our time were experts in understanding how bias works and how it affects people. **Peggy Seeger** and **Loretta Lynn** were two figures who stood up for women's rights in the male-dominated music business earlier in this century. **Sarah McLachlan** is a more recent female pioneer in the music industry because she countered the industry's bias against an all female lineup by organizing the immensely successful Lilith Fair music festival.

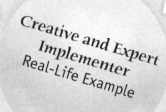

Creative and Expert Implementer Real-Life Example

Ideas for Developing Skills

Level 1: Immersion in Examples and Opportunities
Attend to the big picture, Learn to recognize basic patterns

Extending beyond our own in-groups. Ask students to arrange an interview with someone who is different from themselves (in gender, age, cultural background) and have them design interview questions that will capture their differences (respectfully). Have them also do the same interview with someone who is similar to themselves. Then, have students compare the responses of an in-group member to those of an out-group member (and notice the bias that comes with group membership!). Reinforce the lesson that while it is often easier to communicate with people from our own in-groups, it is rewarding and interesting to communicate outside of those habitual groups that consist of similar people.

Bias toward people with disabilities. Though more and more people are conscientious about preventing racial and gender bias, there is still a great deal of discrimination against people with disabilities. Point out that, particularly with students their age, ignoring someone with a disability can be just as hurtful as teasing them. If appropriate, have students simulate the experience of having a disability (walking around blindfolded, or watching TV with the sound off). This must be done with extreme sensitivity if there are students with disabilities in the classroom so that they don't feel singled out. Try to get their input on how to structure the lesson.

Double standards in history. Present some double standards from different points in history (bias against lefties in ancient times, bias against girl babies in China, bias against freed black slaves in post Civil War America, etc.) and ask students to articulate what is similar about the ways those people were treated, the justification/rationale of those double standards in their communities, and the ways in which social action changed the double standard (if the double standard still exists, ask students to brainstorm on ways that it could be changed).

Starred activities within each subskill go together!

Controlling Social Bias
by Diagnosing It

Ideas for Developing Skills

Level 1 (continued)

"Minnesota Pride, Minnesota Prejudice." Watch the film by this name, which depicts the bias that each ethnic group in Minnesota suffered when they arrived in Minnesota (or when others arrived, as in the case of native Americans). Use the film as a catalyst for discussion about past or current prejudice against these groups.

Why do people hate others? Investigate opinions on why people hate others. Make sure to include sources from criminology, psychology, sociology, philosophy, political science. Have students present their findings. Sources to use include the websites of People of all Races Against Racism, Hatewatch.org, United Against Hate, Anti-defamation League, Southern Poverty Law Center.

Why do people kill other people? Investigate opinions on why people kill others. Make sure to include sources from criminology, psychology, sociology, philosophy, political science. Have students present their findings. Sources to use include the websites of People of all Races Against Racism, Hatewatch.org, United Against Hate, Anti-defamation League, Southern Poverty Law Center.

Level 2: Attention to Facts and Skills
Focus on detail and prototypical knowledge, Build knowledge

Effects of bias. Give students a template and ask them to construct a "chain reaction" table showing how bias can start a negative chain of events. SAMPLE TEMPLATE:
If person A did/said _____, it could make person B feel _____. So person B might _____ and then person A might react by _____.

Spotting bias. Have students watch examples of males and females being treated like objects on video clips and identify the biases they show. As they become more skilled at spotting bias, more subtle examples can be used (many sitcoms are brimming with gender bias as the basis of jokes; i.e., treating men and women as pieces of meat rather than people).

 Gender role equity in literature. These chapter books (some historical) provide a good context in which gender roles can be discussed or written about: *Catherine, Called Birdy*, by K. Cushman; *The Midwife's Apprentice*, by K. Cushman; *You Want Women to Vote, Lizzie Stanton?*, by J. Fritz; *On the Far Side of the Mountain*, by J. George; *The Harvey Girls: The Women Who Civilized the West*, by J. Morris. Some discussion or essay questions include: Who or what made the women take these roles? Would you have done that? When (in everyday life) do you get to pick your role? When do you not get to pick? Could you change that?

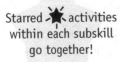
Starred activities within each subskill go together!

ES-5 Controlling Social Bias

Controlling Social Bias
by Diagnosing It

Ideas for Developing Skills

Level 2 (continued)

Bias in everyday design. Ask students to examine the design of the school building and classroom furnishings (e.g., desks, tables) to determine whether or not these designs are biased against left-handed, tall, short, or physically disabled persons.

Find stereotyping. Have students list all the stereotypes they can — positive and negative — about a particular group. Have students discuss whether or not these stereotypes are reflected in the behavior of a character in a story or film, or that of a real-life person (from www.tolerance.org).

Level 3: Practice Procedures
Set goals, Plan steps of problem solving, Practice skills

Advertising Power. Bias is often what makes us prefer one product over another. Any magazine or primetime TV block is full of examples of ads using images of thin, young, attractive people to make us prefer their products. Have students create "typical" advertisements and then identify common elements to discuss the power of advertising in creating and perpetuating bias. The more they exaggerate their ads, the more effective the discussion will be.

Opinion/proof charts. With literature or current/historical events, help students think critically by creating a chart with an 'opinion' column and 'proof' column (see *Multicultural Literacy*, Diamond & Moore, 1995, p. 94 for an example with literature). Examining each opinion with the corresponding proof, especially the ones that contradict each other, can help students realize that bias often involves being selective about the facts we choose to ignore and pay attention to. Consideration of all the facts is one way to minimize bias.

Test for automatic bias. Have students learn about automatic bias through a jigsaw activity (see the Appendix) using the information available at www.tolerance.org. Then have each take one or more of the automatic bias tests available at www.tolerance.org. You can select any one (or more) of these topics: black/white bias, arab/muslim bias, skin tone bias, age bias, gender bias, weight bias. Each person gets their results immediately after taking the test. Ask students to write down anonymously their test results. Afterwards, discuss the results of the class and specific steps the class can take to counter the biases they discovered.

Controlling Social Bias by Diagnosing It

Ideas for Developing Skills

Level 3 (continued)

Bias in math. Use real-world examples to show students creative ways in which people (other than university-educated, intellectual theorists) have developed math for practical reasons (i.e., Brazilian street children using unconventional procedures for computing change when selling Candy; see *Common Bonds*, Byrnes & Kiger, 1996, p. 95 for other examples). Discuss why we tend to be biased toward our own conventional methods and regard certain methods as better than others. Another everyday comparison to discuss is our tendency to think that computers do everything better (banking, grocery checkout, educational testing). Challenge the students to think of times when the computers can fail.

Confronting bias in sports. Read excerpts from an account of minorities in sports, such as McKissack and McKissack's (1994) *Black Diamond: The Story of the Negro Baseball Leagues*, and ask students to compare this period's race issues to modern day race issues. Also include discussions of disabled persons and women in sports.

Level 4: Integrate Knowledge and Procedures *Execute plans, Solve problems*

Ideals. Have students compare lists of "what is good" or "what is ideal" to different groups and discuss how these value differences affect the way we view situations and conflicts. For example, take a situation that threatens one group's most highly regarded value (like a sports team losing its fans) and compare how different culture groups, different school organizations, different groups in the community, different political groups, and/or people with different educational backgrounds might react differently because they don't hold the same ideals.

Assessment Hints

Diagnose bias

Journal. Students write about instances of bias that they have observed.

Chart. Students use graphic displays to illustrate cycles or habits that tend to contribute to bias and misunderstanding.

Individual performance. Following a cooperative or class activity targeting a particular sensitivity skill, students are assessed on their individual performance using a new example.

Controlling Social Bias by Overcoming It

Virginia Foster Durr is one of 23 real-life moral exemplars in the book *Some Do Care: Contemporary Lives of Moral Commitment* (Colby & Damon, 1992). Mrs. Durr came from a Southern aristocratic white family. She grew up with the belief that African Americans were innately inferior to white people. Mrs. Durr, however, changed her beliefs about African Americans with new experiences in college and throughout her career. Later, Mrs. Durr played an important role in the fight for civil rights for African Americans in the 1960s.

Ideas for Developing Skills

Level 1: Immersion in Examples and Opportunities
Attend to the big picture, Learn to recognize basic patterns

Lack of critical thinking in our entertainment choices. Take an anonymous poll of students' favorite movies over the past year. Some time later, ask students to reflect on the violence in our society and how they feel about it. Depending on what their responses look like, lead the students through a reflective discussion of how similar or dissimilar their movie choices are compared to their ideals (feelings about real-life violence). Why are we drawn to violent media and how does it affect us as individuals and as a society? What kind of people do we tend to admire as heroes? What small choices can we make in our everyday lives to try not to be part of this bias toward violence? How can we move our bias and expectations more toward peaceful conflict resolution?

Level 2: Attention to Facts and Skills
Focus on detail and prototypical knowledge, Build knowledge

What can we do about bias? Have students watch video clips of sitcoms in groups and work together to identify incidences of bias (gender, age, body shape, cultural, etc.) and reflect on how things could have been said or done differently to control bias.

Practice in controlling bias. Have students examine a school document (such as dress code policy or honor code) for bias and rewrite the document as needed.

How to keep from hating others. Have students connect with the youth group Student Alliance for Equality (through their website, for example) and read their list of 100 ways to combat prejudice. Have students select one or more of the suggestions to implement. You can try implementing several over the course of a semester.

Controlling Social Bias
by Overcoming It

Ideas for Developing Skills

Level 2 (continued)

Pledge against prejudice. Have students create a pledge against prejudice (or use the one at the Student Alliance for Equality website) that they will all sign and post in the classroom.

Level 3: Practice Procedures
Set goals, Plan steps of problem solving, Practice skills

Confronting bias in science. Teaching science in a "science, technology, and society" approach can tackle issues of how bias in science may be used to rationalize things powerful people do at the expense of less powerful people, such as pollution, plant growth, propagation, and harvesting (see *Common Bonds,* Byrnes & Kiger, p.97 for other examples).

Helping others to not hate others. Have students take their pledge against prejudice (from Level 2) to other students and community members to sign.

Level 4: Integrate Knowledge and Procedures
Execute plans, Solve problems

Bias in student-created cultures. As part of a larger discussion of values and differences, ask students to create descriptions of what an ideal culture would be like. Discuss how they would control bias in this ideal culture.

Confront prejudice. Write letters to leaders who are intolerant or exhibit prejudice behavior.

Act against bias in your school. Take a survey of bias in the school. Use the findings to create an action plan to make changes.

Community Campaign against bias. Some people have helped raise awareness of bias in their communities by pointing out disparities in access to social services, good education, voting, good jobs, transportation to work and school, etc. Select one issue and get some numbers to support your arguments that change should be made. Make a flyer to use in a social action campaign.

Controlling Social Bias
by Overcoming It

Ideas for Developing Skills

Level 4 (continued)

What is it really like? Find books that describe the life of the poor. For example, read *Nickled and Dimed*, by Barbara Ehrenreich, a journalist who writes about her attempt to survive on minimum wage jobs across the country. Or read *Worlds Apart* by Cynthia Duncan which describes three different poor areas of the country, finding a lack of democracy and opportunity in two of them. Propose some "what if?" scenarios to challend them to build a bias-free society. The point of this activity is to acknowledge that bias is part of human nature, but realize that it can be countered with conscious effort.

Counter stereotypes. Using photos from magazines or a pre-organized collection (such as that in *Turning on Learning*, Grant & Sleeter, 1998, pp. 60-61) have students select words or phrases that might describe a person from a stereotyped group (e.g., garbage collectors, migrant workers, inner-city teenagers, homeless families). In a manner appropriate to your particular classroom atmosphere, have students confront their own biases privately or in group(s). They should reflect on where they got the ideas that contributed to their stereotypes and then make conscious efforts to imagine and/or seek out exceptions to those stereotypes.

Assessment Hints

Overcome bias

Communications. Have students write reports, posters, public service announcements, or speeches, describing biases that need to be overcome by others.

Social action projects. Have students create and participate in social action projects that deal with issues of bias. Project ideas include petitions, demonstrations, letter writing, advocacy, and campaigning.

Controlling Social Bias by Nurturing Tolerance

Creative and Expert Implementer Real-Life Example

Senator *J. William Fulbright* is best known for the scholarship program (for scholars to work in another country) named after him. He designed the Fulbright Program to, as he said, "bring a little more knowledge, a little more reason, and a little more compassion into world affairs and thereby to increase the chance that nations will learn at last to live in peace and friendship."

Ideas for Developing Skills

Level 1: Immersion in Examples and Opportunities
Attend to the big picture, Learn to recognize basic patterns

Tolerance does not mean to 'bear with' something you dislike or despise. Tolerance is a personal decision that comes from a belief that every person is a treasure (from www.tolerance.org). It is the appreciation of diversity and its importance.

Everyone is a minority. Introduce students to the broad conceptualization of being a minority. Have you ever been the only one in your group of friends who liked a particular song? Have you ever been the only one in your family to like a particular food? Is it OK for you to hold a minority position? Have students discuss or write in response to this challenge, "If I tried to talk you out of your minority position, how would you stick up for it?"

Survey school's support for diversity. Have students read about tolerance and fighting prejudice at www.tolerance.org (a jigsaw activity could work nicely—see Appendix). Then have them take an inventory of the school. How does the school support diversity (e.g., bilingual announcements) and how does it not (e.g., special dietary needs in the cafeteria). Provide a summary report to the administration and/or to the school as a whole (e.g., through the school newspaper).

Calendar diversity. If the school does not have a calendar that lists he religious and cultural holidays of its students and staff, have students put one together. Students investigate what cultural and religious groups are represented at the school. Then they investigate their major holidays. Ask the school administration to include this information in their yearly, monthly, and weekly calendars, and to respect religious holidays by not scheduling important events on those days.

Explore diversity. Have students try out things from other cultures, or example: (1) Music: have students listen to music from different (non-Western) cultures. (2) Food: Bring in food that students have not tried for them to taste. (3) Stories: Have students read stories from other countries. (4) Art: Have students look at art from other countries.

Controlling Social Bias by Nurturing Tolerance

Ideas for Developing Skills

Level 2: Attention to Facts and Skills
Focus on detail and prototypical knowledge, Build knowledge

Lessons from the civil rights movement on how to confront bias. Find accounts written by first hand participants in the civil rights movement, such as King and Osborne's (1997) *Oh Freedom!: Kids Talk About the Civil Rights Movement with People Who Made it Happen*. Based on the accounts, ask students to construct a "recipe" for confronting bias, listing what you need and the steps to go through. There is no one right way, but this is a fairly concrete way to begin discussing a complex topic. Bumper stickers. After any lesson on confronting bias, have students construct bumper stickers or banners with "take home" messages. Put them up around the classroom and reinforce the messages as other situations/discussions arise.

Bumper stickers. After any lesson on confronting bias, have students construct bumper stickers or banners with "take home" messages. Put them up around the classroom and reinforce the messages as other situations/discussions arise.

Pledge for tolerance. Have students sign the pledge at www.tolerance.org (101 tools for tolerance). Have students post the pledge in the classroom or in the school hallway. Have students recruit other students to sign the pledge.

Pen Pals. Set up a pen pal relationship with students or a classroom from another country.

Accessibility. Have students investigate how accessible the school grounds are. Organize a class project to help the school reach compliance with the American for Disabilities Act.

Examine the costs of intolerance. Using math and science skills, put together statistics, graphs and figures of the costs of one form of intolerance. Make a poster to hang in the hallway or discuss your findings at a school assembly.

Level 3: Practice Procedures
Set goals, Plan steps of problem solving, Practice skills

Confronting bias in social studies. Have students research heroes and "sheroes" from history including those belonging to marginalized groups like people with disabilities, ethnic minorities, children, etc. Then ask them to create visual art or poetry representing the heroes' acts and put these up around the classroom to help reinforce these untypical images of heroes. Help the students realize that not all heroes are powerful people and that anyone who rises to the occasion can be brave and do good things.

Starred activities within each subskill go together!

Controlling Social Bias by Nurturing Tolerance

Ideas for Developing Skills

Level 3 (continued)

Good sportsmanship. Have students investigate the behavior of fans at inter-school competitions. Have them investigate how good sportsmanship can be promoted (e.g., applaud the other team).

Library books. Have students investigate how diverse the school's library (or classroom's) books are. Are there books that include people of different ethnicity, age, weight, socio-economic status?

Webquest for tolerance. Have students complete a webquest activity. Choose one from a list at http://webquest.sdsu.edu/.

One-world mural for tolerance. Have students (all ages) add to the one-world on-line mural at www.tolerance.org. A lesson plan is there.

Level 4: Integrate Knowledge and Procedures
Execute plans, Solve problems

Making media recommendations for younger kids. Use popular TV programs or ads to reflect on the bias of media and the "tools" of media (how they use sex and violence to get people to pay attention). Ask students to reflect on the media's impact on younger kids and which kinds of content they would or wouldn't allow younger kids to watch. This is to help develop a monitoring perspective that would ideally carry into their own viewing.

Sponsor a fair. Sponsor an international fair or bazaar. Bring in international music, food, products. Invite the community.

Organize a rally. Read short stories or poems by minority groups at a community rally for tolerance. Ask the high school drama teacher, local actor, or director to coach students on performing.

Take social action to meet needs. Increase tolerance in the community by petitioning for increased access where it is needed, more language translators and teachers, more ethnic restaurants and grocery stores.

Assessment Hints

Nurture tolerance

Journal. Students write about the small (or big!) ways in which they are going to try to prevent bias.

Produce "bumper stickers." Students create bumper stickers that accurately capture ideas on how to control prejudice and social bias.

Chart. Students use graphic displays to illustrate cycles or habits that tend to contribute to bias and misunderstanding.

Individual performance. Following a cooperative or class activity targeting a particular sensitivity skill, students are assessed on their individual performance using a new example.

Create a Climate
to Develop Skills in Controlling Bias

Ideas for Learning Control of Social Bias in the Classroom

Stopping cruelty. When a student is ostracized because of unusual dress or smell or behavior, one must perform a mediation to help the class change its behavior and attitude. Select a mediator from outside the classroom (e.g., a special needs teacher) or take the role yourself. When the ostracized student is not present, do the following. On the chalkboard, draw one circle representing the ostracized student on one side. On the other side draw many circles to represent the individuals and draw a large circle around this group of circles. Between the large group and the ostracized circle and the large circle filled with many circles, draw yourself as a line, a "mirror" or mediator. If the student has a disability, discuss what it is and what it is like. Then ask the students for their feelings toward the ostracized student. Ask how they think the ostracized student feels. Discuss how their behavior is affecting the rejected student. ("It may not be visible to you, but you are hurting her. You are convincing her that she is the kind of person that people don't like, that she is worthless. These ideas will stay in her head for many years to come and affect her ability to succeed socially or in other ways.") If the students are scapegoating the student, discuss this with them. Finally, ask if they want to continue their behavior toward the student or change it. (This is adapted from Lickona, 1991, pp. 97-8.) Lickona suggests not to give up even if the class is resistant to change at first; remember to appeal to their minds and hearts; avoid these problems by developing an ethical classroom climate from the beginning.

Racism and other "isms." If someone makes a statement against an individual because of their group membership or generalizes about members of groups, we suggest that you do the following. (NOTE: These DOs and DON'Ts are from *Unity in Diversity: A Curriculum Resource Guide For Ethno-Cultural Equity And Anti-Racist Education*, Ontario Ministry of Education, 1991).

DO THESE THINGS
when you witness racism or other "isms":

- Deal with the situation IMMEDIATELY.
- State that such abuse is HARMFUL and will not be tolerated.
- VALUE the feelings of others by listening with sensitivity.
- SUPPORT the victim.
- TAKE ASIDE those involved to discuss the incident.
- APPLY APPROPRIATE CONSEQUENCES to the offender.
- EXAMINE THE CONTEXT for subtle support of such offenses.

DON'T DO THESE THINGS
when you witness racism or other "isms":

- Don't IGNORE it, let it pass unchallenged, or let intangible fear block your ability to act.
- Don't OVERREACT with a put-down of the offender.
- Don't IMPOSE CONSEQUENCES until you know what happened from everyone involved.
- Don't focus entirely on the offender; REMEMBER THE VICTIM.
- Don't EMBARRASS either party publicly.
- Don't ASSUME THE INCIDENT IS ISOLATED from the context in which it occurred.

Sample Student Self-Monitoring
Controlling Social Bias

Encourage active learning by having students learn to monitor their own learning

Diagnose bias

Where did I get my expectations?

Where did I get my values?

I work to identify and overcome my prejudices.

I notice bias in the media.

Overcome bias

What do I see?

Does someone else want me to think this way for a reason?

Could I have misinterpreted the situation?

Am I being objective?

Is there another way I could interpret this situation?

Nurture tolerance

I am patient with others.

It is all right for people to do things differently from me.

I enjoy the differences among students in my classroom.

I am interested in different ways of seeing things.

It doesn't matter what a person looks like on the outside, it's

what's inside that counts.

I can get along well with different kinds of people.

Interpreting Situations

(Create choices)

WHAT

Interpreting situations involves developing the creative skills used in generating multiple interpretations of a situation and multiple alternatives for dealing with it. It also means having the skills to counter normal pitfalls in intersocial interpretation. This is a critical step in any kind of problem solving. People often repeat the same mistakes because they respond automatically without considering another way to behave.

WHY

This is a critical step in any kind of problem solving. People often repeat the same mistakes because they have not considered another way to behave.

SUBSKILLS

1: Determine what is happening

2: Perceive morality

Categories of interpretations: how perceptions might differ for another individual, another culture, a different generation, opposite sex, different SES, different neighborhood, different country, different ability, veteran status, sexual orientation, type of expert (e.g., artist vs. engineer). Situations/actions relevant to middle schoolers: Drug use, alcohol use, smoking, shopping, breaking a rule, doing homework, family responsibili-ties, behaving in class, re-specting adults, treatment of peers, grooming, recreational choices, loyalty.

3: Respond creatively

ES-6 Interpreting Situations

Web Wise

See www.rippleeffects.com for youth oriented information about personal effects on others

Find many resources for teaching creative thinking at:

http://www.teachers.ash.org.au/researchskills/thinking.htm

Creative problem solving tips and activities: http://www.ncdini.org/

Interpreting Situations
by Determining What is Happening

Rachel Carson, a marine biologist, environmentalist, and writer, helped shape environmental consciousness by being one of the first to determine what was happening. During the 1950s and 1960s, Rachel Carson conducted research on and wrote about the harmful effects of pesticides on the food chain.

Ideas for Developing Skills

Level 1: Immersion in Examples and Opportunities
Attend to the big picture, Learn to recognize basic patterns

Humor and multiple interpretations. One of the classic methods used by TV script writers to make us laugh is by showing us a situation that looks a particular way to one person and completely different to another person. Just about any kids' joke book includes the same type of humor (based on misunderstanding or puns with double meanings). Share some of these examples with students to help them start to think about multiple interpretations in a fun way.

Generational differences. Have students interview community elders to find out which things they think young and old people have different opinions of and why.

Sherlock Holmes. Use mysteries, short stories (e.g., by Borges) or nonfiction written like a mystery to help students practice keeping track of many facts in order to determine what is happening.

Working with partial information. To sharpen students' observational skills, watch a show or film clip without the sound and ask students to determine what is happening. Do the same with just the sound and no picture. Use examples that have interpersonal conflict.

Level 2: Attention to Facts and Skills
Focus on detail and prototypical knowledge, Build knowledge

Local differences. Invite a local leader in to discuss the different perspectives that local citizens have on some key issues (or bring in a panel of people with different opinions).

Interpreting Situations
by Determining What is Happening

Ideas for Developing Skills

Level 2 (continued)

Ways to interpret interpersonal situations. Examine how different people tend to interpret interpersonal situations. For example, bullies and aggressive people tend to think that other people are out to get them and turn neutral behavior (someone accidentally bumping them) into a threat. Find examples in television, movies, magazines or books.

Breakthroughs. Some people are able to piece many bits of information together to create a revolutionary theory or perspective (although they are usually building on other people's work, too). Study one or more of these people (e.g., Picasso, Martha Graham, Bob Fosse, Plato, Aristotle, Ford, Einstein).

What is happening in my domain? Invite speakers to talk about how they keep up with the information of their domain, how they determine what is happening in their line of work, and about what information they do not have. For example, researchers read published and pre-published articles about similar work by other researchers. They look for solid, replicated evidence. The information they do not have is what does not get published— the experiments that failed. Other speakers could be from the arts, politics, civic leadership, engineers, farmers, and so on.

Level 3: Practice Procedures
Set goals, Plan steps of problem solving, Practice skills

Which interpretations do people favor? Using the items from the scavenger hunt (see above activity in Level 2), have students interview several people to see which interpretation(s) are more likely to be used. Lead students in a discussion of times when unlikely interpretations are sometimes true.

Giving people the benefit of the doubt. When you're in the habit of generating multiple interpretations, you're less likely to jump to conclusions. Present the students with several interpersonal dilemmas, such as "James rams his shoulder into you in the hallway and doesn't say anything." and "Joanna tells you she'll call you and then doesn't." Ask the students to think of all the possible reasons why the person might have behaved that way and help them practice giving the other person the benefit of the doubt. See the Appendix for some short interpersonal dilemmas.

Silent film. Watch a film without the sound and have the class try to guess what the characters are saying and doing. Select a film in which there are likely to be many ambiguous scenes.

Interpreting Situations
by Determining What is Happening

Ideas for Developing Skills

Level 3 (continued)

Points of view. People's point of view about a situation or defining a problem often differ depending on a number of factors. Discuss scenarios, dilemmas, or community problems from these different viewpoints: (a) Inside view (it's happening to me), outside view (it's happening to someone else). (b) Power view (I have decision making power financial power, political power), powerless view (things are being done that are out of my control). (c) In-group view (it's my family, my social group), out-group view (I'm on the outside of the in-crowd).

How people interpret political situations. Take several community or national issues and investigate attitudes from different parts of the political spectrum. Write down their opinion about what should be done and the rationale they give. Make sure you know who is funding the opinion makers you read. The funders' viewpoints are usually the ones you hear. Analyze the facts and discuss whether or not the full picture is taken into account by any one perspective. Then put together your own full-picture analysis. Perspectives: (a) left/alternative, (b) right/powerful, (c) center/moderate.

Level 4: Integrate Knowledge and Procedures
Execute plans, Solve problems

What is happening in the community? An interdisciplinary project. Here is an exercise to improve student intuitions about their community. (1) Ask students how healthy they think their community is. Take a rating or grade as a pre-test. (2) Ask students what information they need to make a better decision. Who are the members of the community? Who keeps track of what kind of information about the different groups? What other kind of data provide information that helps us in our analysis. The list should include at least economic, health, welfare, employment, educational outcomes. (3) Have students gather the information. Divide the task among small groups. (4) Have the groups put their information together. They should have data, narrative information, and perhaps their own surveys or analyses. (5) Put the information together in a readable format. (6) Have students rate or grade the health of the community. (7) Invite local leaders to read the report (or see the posters, whatever format was used) and provide feedback. The leaders should point out what available information is missing (and perhaps why the students didn't get it), what information is unavailable that would be helpful, and what they think of the grade the students gave. (8) Revise the report, put it into a flyer, and distribute the information to the local community. (9) Use the information as a catalyst to take action to solve a local problem that was identified.

Interpreting Situations
by Determining What is Happening

Ideas for Developing Skills

Level 4 (continued)

Political paranoia. Why is it so easy to convince people of the blame-worthiness of an out-group? Political psychologists attribute it to the natural human propensity to blame someone else when we feel vulnerable or helpless. It helps us feel stronger and focused, on the enemy. Study situations in which leaders exploited their people by powerfully showing the threat of an 'enemy' (e.g., Hitler, Pol Pot in Cambodia, the Mei Lai incident in Vietnam, Idi Amin of Uganda, Milosovic of the former Yugoslavia, Stalin). What threats did they identify? How real were the threats (according to you and those who have analyzed the situation)? Do their words and actions look like anything occurring around the world today? Where? Write an essay or give a speech.

Assessment Hints

Determine What Is Happening

Generate multiple interpretations. Alone or within a group, students generate multiple interpretations for a situation.

Essays. Students write creative essays on real or hypothetical dilemmas, coming up with innovative ways of looking at the problem (like seeing the possible good in a negative situation).

Reports. Have students write reports on research findings.

Speeches. Have students give speeches based on a full reading and understanding of the problem.

Essays. Have students write essays describing different perspectives.

ES-6 Interpreting Situations

Interpreting Situations by Perceiving Morality

Creative and Expert Implementer Real-Life Example

Albert Schweitzer, internationally known organist, theologian, and scholar, dedicated his life to mankind and became an international symbol of humanitarianism, his name synonymous with altruism. He founded a hospital in Lambarene, Africa to fight malaria and leprosy, then used his prize money from the 1952 Nobel Peace Award to treat leprosy. While working in Africa, Schweitzer wrote an ethical philosophy called "reverence for life" that emphasized the preciousness of all living things. He would not even slap a mosquito.

Ideas for Developing Skills

Level 1: Immersion in Examples and Opportunities
Attend to the big picture, Learn to recognize basic patterns

Attuning the senses to moral information. Show students paintings and photos that have moral significance. Ask them to identify the features that make it of moral significance. Use very obvious selections (e.g., Guernica by Picasso depicts death and suffering in many forms) and more subtle selections (e.g., murals by Diego Rivera). Then show pictures from books and magazines and have students discuss whether or not there is anything morally relevant in them.

How do you see it? Read about a situation from the perspective of the winner/conquerer and also from the perspective of victims or the oppressed (e.g., the discovery of America, atomic bombing of Hiroshima and Nagasaki, Exxon Valdez oil spill, the Tuskegee experiment, nuclear testing in the 1950s in the western U.S.). Discuss what is the same about their perspectives and what differs.

Look for moral meaning. In everyday school work, look for moral implications. For example: *Science*: If scientists clone people, what does that mean for human well-being? *Math*: We can use numbers to support the social action we are planning. *Literature*: How does this story improve our moral imagination, envisioning the possible actions and outcomes? *Social studies*: What is a way we could solve this problem if it happens again? *Physical education*: Does it matter if I cheat?

Learn from the past. Find examples of heroes who were inspired by the positive or negative effects of others. For example, Hugh Thompson was one of the soldiers who tried to protect the Vietnamese civilians at Mei Lai when Lt. Calley led the massacre of the whole village. He said one of the reasons he helped was that he remembered that the Nazis had done similar things.

Starred ★ activities within each subskill go together!

Interpreting Situations
by Perceiving Morality

Ideas for Developing Skills

Level 1 (continued)

It's the little things. Investigate (using the internet) and discuss the following topics. Have students write essays or create posters for the school based on what they learn.

(1) <u>Teasing</u>. When is teasing bullying? Is bullying ever okay? Why?

(2) <u>Putdowns</u>. What is a putdown? What does it do for the one who gives it? How does it affect the receiver? What is the result when it happens a lot?

(3) <u>Cliques of the ups and the downs</u>. What is good and bad about cliques? Are there cliques in our school? How can we prevent cliques from being too strong and harmful?

(4) <u>Foot in the door</u>. What little things should we watch out for everyday? What things should we try not to do and what should we call others to account on? The village of Chambon was led by leaders and citizens who defied the authority of the Nazi take-over of France. They did not salute the flag representing occupation, they did not sign an unconditional oath swearing allegiance to the new government. And they ended up hiding over 5,000 Jews during the course of the war. They didn't let the Nazis get a foot in the door—a technique that worked for the Nazis elsewhere—for example in the Netherlands when the Nazis asked for a list of Jews that should not be deported (all were scheduled for deportation eventually).

(5) <u>Watch out for smoke and mirrors</u>. The Nazis tried to keep everyone confused about what they were really doing by using language that masked the true intent, or by promising something and retracting it in action. How does this happen today? What should citizens watch out for?

(6) <u>All for all.</u> Keeping self-respect and respect for others at all times can prevent a lot of harm. Discuss how the whole city of Amsterdam went on strike after the Nazis brutally rounded up 400 Jews for deportation.

(7) <u>Ordinary everyday decency can grow into a heroic act</u>. Read about the villagers of Le Chambon who acted in ordinary ways to save the lives of Jews. How can you be decent every day?

Level 2: Attention to Facts and Skills
Focus on detail and prototypical knowledge, Build knowledge

Causal chains. Examine effects of people on people. This could be in a particular domain or in general. Have students reflect and write on questions like the following.

(1) Who does things that affect me (in general, at lunch, after school)? How do they affect me? Whom else do they affect?

(2) How do I affect others (in general, in class, at home)? Whom do I affect? Whom do those people affect?

Starred ★ activities within each subskill go together!

Interpreting Situations
by Perceiving Morality

Ideas for Developing Skills

Level 2 (continued)

Paying attention to the cues. Look at a particular domain and examine the cues important for success in the situation or problem. Here are some examples. Have students investigate and /or invite a speaker.

Rescue workers. What do rescue workers and rescue dogs look for when searching for person alive in rubble? What are the cues that lead them to dig in a certain place?

Good parents. What do parents pay attention to when they are with their children? What cues do they look for to know that everything is okay? What cues tell them that something is wrong?

Whistle blowers. Investigate the cues that whistle blowers pay attention to that others miss or ignore. Why do the whistle blowers speak up? Why do they take a risk?

Other domains could be farmers, teachers, nurses, doctors, police officers, artists, athletes.

Circle of concern. A circle of concern is a metaphor for all the things we care about preserving and protecting. Each student should think about the following questions and draw their circle of concern. Students should also list the things that they don't care about. Follow each section of questions with a discussion.

(1) <u>Be aware of your circle of concern</u>. Draw your circle of concern as you answer these questions. What is in your circle of concern, what do you care about? Do you care about your family and friends only? Do you extend your concern to other people? Which ones? Do you include your community in your circle? How about your city, state, country? Do you include people from other countries in your circle? Do you include only people or do you include other living things? Where do you draw the line? What don't you care about? What could someone throw from a mountain top and you wouldn't care? Are there other things you care about?

(2) <u>Vulnerabilities of your circle of concern</u>. Now think about all the people and things included in your circle of concern. How are they vulnerable? What can hurt them? Are they always vulnerable? When are they not vulnerable?

(3) <u>Protecting your circle of concern</u>. How do you want the people and things in your circle of concern to be treated? How do you think other people should treat them?

(4) <u>Unconcerned</u>. Look at your list of things that you don't care about. Why don't you care about them? How are they different from the things in your circle of concern? (Be very specific.)

(5) <u>Inclusion</u>. Who do you think would put you in their circle of concern? Why?

(6) <u>Exclusion</u>. Who do you think would put you on their 'don't care about' list? Why? What would the people on your 'don't care about list' think about you? Are they being fair?

(7) <u>Unconcerned reconsidered</u>. Look again at the things and people on your 'don't care about' list. Do you still feel the same way? Are you being fair?

Interpreting Situations
by Perceiving Morality

Ideas for Developing Skills

Level 2 (continued)

Morality in a particular domain. Investigate issues of moral impact from work done in a particular domain (e.g., fast food restaurant workers, newspaper journalists). Invite an expert speaker. Use these criteria: (1) Is there an immediate direct effect on other people or the planet? (2) Is there a delayed direct effect on other people or the planet? (3) Is the work part of a multi-person creation that results in a product or outcome that has positive or negative effects?

What are the moral implications? Does morality mean no negative impact? Or does it require a positive impact? Is it possible to have a neutral impact?

Failing to see. Read a story or play like *The Lottery* (by S. Jackson), which depicts the consequences of not acting on moral instinct and how moral instinct can die from peer pressure.

Defiant goodness. Study what happened in Le Chambon, a small village in Nazi-occupied France. 5,000 citizens sheltered 5,000 Jews, protecting them from persecution and death. For information about a movie and books, and for more information, see www.chambon.org.

Level 3: Practice Procedures
Set goals, Plan steps of problem solving, Practice skills

Monitor susceptibilities and limitations. There are many things that can be a source of bias and make us less interested in helping someone. Here are a few. Discuss examples and ways to overcome your own unconscious reaction.
   (a) <u>Cultural linguistic</u> (differences in accent or grammar). Diagnose what bias you have toward a person's speech and then work against your prejudice by listening to someone you like and thinking positively about their sound.
   (b) <u>Attention to movement & sound</u>. We are distracted by movement and sound—our eyes want to immediately look at where it came from (this is why advertisers of products and movies use a lot of flashing and noise). Practice being in the room with the television on and resisting the inclination to look. This skill is important in situations where someone might need your help and other things threaten to distract your attention.
   (c) <u>Mood and idea priming</u>. Humans are susceptible to carrying over their feelings from a previous situation to a new situation and misattributing it to the new situation.

ES-6 Interpreting Situations

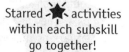

Starred activities within each subskill go together!

Interpreting Situations by Perceiving Morality

Ideas for Developing Skills

Assessment Hints

Level 3 (continued)

Interact with others in the situation. One of the ways to stay empathetic with others is to notice and pay attention to them. In experiments where an actor pretended to be a victim, people would help if they had looked the victim in the eye. People who didn't share eye contact did not help.

Broaden your sensitivities in a domain. Have students read widely, many opinions and perspectives, in order to stimulate sensitivity to more things. Test their growth with pre and post problem solving in the domain.

Level 4: Integrate Knowledge and Procedures
Execute plans, Solve problems

What is my role in the situation? Present everyday scenarios and ask students to discuss what their role is. Then role play the scenarios. Ask students to act similarly in real life when those or similar situations arise.

What are the opportunities for action? Lead students through a visualization where they imagine their typical school day. Ask students to write down all the encounters they have on a usual day, from big to small. Then have them imagine themselves in each situation and what moral choices they have. For example, are they using too much water to brush their teeth or take a shower? Did they take too much cereal and throw some away? Did they ignore their baby sister? Did they not help their mother carry a heavy load to the car? And so on, through the day. (You may want to take just part of a day.) Once they have identified morally relevant actions or inactions, ask them to think about it and act on them the next few days, keeping track of what they do. After a couple of weeks ask them to visually scan their usual day and see if anything has changed.

Deal with Ambiguity

Reflective activities. Have students write reflective essays or keep a report diary on situations they encounter that have moral implications.

Dialogue journal. Have students keep a dialogue journal (you write back to the student). Students keep track of and write about situations which have moral implications.

Literature journal. Have students keep a response-to-literature journal in which they reflect on the literature that they are reading and how the characters perceive moral situations.

Simulated journal. Have students keep a simulated journal of a person living in the past. They imagine what moral situations this person encountered.

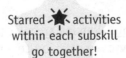

Starred activities within each subskill go together!

Interpreting Situations by Responding Creatively

Creative and Expert Implementer Real-Life Example

Bob Dylan is known for his creative response to the 1960s U.S. political mainstream culture. His criticism, embedded in poetic songs, established him as the definitive songwriter of the '60s protest movement.

Ideas for Developing Skills

Level 1: Immersion in Examples and Opportunities
Attend to the big picture, Learn to recognize basic patterns

Multiple interpretations in art. Ask students to bring in or talk about a piece of art that they like. Set these up in a "gallery" and ask students to go through the gallery and choose several pieces of art that they interpret a certain way. Once each student has had a chance to interpret several pieces, arrange for them to share their interpretations with the student who brought that piece in. The goal is to reinforce that multiple interpretations is a major feature that differentiates art from ordinary objects.

More than one possibility in dilemma resolution. Choose an ethical dilemma that allows several possible options for resolution and then present the dilemma to the students, including a description of how one person resolved the dilemma. Then ask the students if that was the only possible way to deal with the situation. Present several dilemmas and return to the question of whether there is usually just one way to resolve a situation.

Examples from history. Investigate the history of conflict between peoples and find examples of creative problem solving (e.g., the underground railroad to free slaves).

Examples from domains. Select a domain and look at its history. When did innovations take place? What are they? How does it happen? How is its encouraged or discourage? Invite a speaker to discuss these matters.

Enter literature. Have students read a story about a kid their age who is faced by an ethical dilemma (e.g., being tempted to cheat) and before they read the ending, discuss other options the kid has. If appropriate, discuss the motivational issues that often keep people from considering all the options, like the tendency to let the burden fall on someone else rather than taking personal responsibility and the tendency to ignore possible consequences.

Interpreting Situations
by Responding Creatively

Ideas for Developing Skills

Level 1 (continued)

How do creative people help the common good? Find examples of artists locally, nationally, internationally from the present and the past who have brought peace or expression to their communities. Here are some specific types of artists to seek out. (a) Examine the life of street artists who perform and work in public. How do they help the community? (b) Read the works of the national poet laureate of the past as well as of the current poet laureate. How do they help the nation? (c) Find examples of music that was composed to express deep human feeling (e.g., *Symphony of Sorrows* by Gorecki, *Fanfare to the Common Man* by Copland). Play the music, write about your reaction, read about the reactions of others in the past. (e) Find murals that have been painted in your town or in towns nearby. What was the point being expressed by the mural? Are there places in your town where a mural might help the community? (f) Community gardens. Does your town have community gardens or parks that are tended by the neighbors? Do you have an abandoned lot that would uplift community spirit if it were planted with flowers?

Level 2: Attention to Facts and Skills
Focus on detail and prototypical knowledge, Build knowledge

Scavenger hunt for things that can be interpreted multiple ways. As individuals or in teams, ask students to find examples of humor, photographs, artwork, or news items that can be interpreted in more than one way.

Talk back to the television. Practice watching a news show or advertisements and challenging the assumptions being made by talking back to the television as a member of a particular group (one sex or the other, poor, elderly, cultural-ethnic group, etc.). In pairs or small groups, let the students practice being interactive with media rather than passive.

Options for using resources. Have students research a few situations in which there are conflicts over resource use. Resources can be natural, monetary, personal time, shared community facilities, etc. Have the students discuss and write about possible options for using the resources responsibly.

Different resource options in different countries. Have students interview community members who come from other countries about options for natural resource usage in their former country and this country. Students can ask questions like: What resources did you have there? Which were the most precious? How did you conserve the most precious resources? Which resources were abundant? How did people conserve these? What cultural values are reflected in resource usage? What conflicts are there over resource usage? What differences do you see with resource usage here?

Interpreting Situations
by Responding Creatively

Ideas for Developing Skills

Level 2 (continued)

Differences in natural resource use across history. Have students research resource usage in other time periods. They can write about what resources were abundant, which were scarce, and how this affected the options available to people. They can also consider questions like: How did people conserve these? What cultural values are reflected in resource usage? What conflicts were there over resource usage? How were resources squandered?

Options for action. Choose an ethical dilemma that allows at least two straightforward options for resolution and ask students to generate at least two options for resolution.

Practice creative responses.
(a) Tell jokes. Have them find and memorize five lighthearted jokes they can use for different situations. Have students practice telling the jokes.
(b) Use silly humor. Find examples of silly humor to bring to class (e.g., Monty Python). Encourage students to use silly humor when things get tense. Used properly, it can defuse anger.
(c) Use puppets to discuss difficult topics. Children and adults will say to puppets what they wouldn't say to each other.
(d) Use drawing and painting to express difficult feelings. This is a good way to get out the feelings that we can't express in words.

Study creative approaches to social problems. Step outside mainstream culture to get a viewpoint about what is happening today. Here are some "outside" sources:
(1) Adbusters is a magazine seeks to shake up the advertising world: http://www.adbusters.org/
(2) The Four Directions is organized to encourage conversation among community members: http://www.fromthefourdirections.org/
(3) The Sustainable Communities Network has many links to local and international groups: http://www.sustainable.org/
(4) The Global Eco-village Network: http://www.gaia.org/
(5) The LOKA Institute is an organization that seeks to make technology and science more responsive to democratically decided social and environmental concerns: http://www.loka.org/
(5) The Asset-Based Community Development Institute (ABCD): http://www.northwestern.edu/ipr/abcd.html

Level 3: Practice Procedures
Set goals, Plan steps of problem solving, Practice skills

Group decision-making. Have students practice group decision making with specific issues to practice hearing all the possible options before evaluating any of them.

Interpreting Situations
by Responding Creatively

Ideas for Developing Skills

Level 3 (continued)

Resource use as a citizen of the world. Have students discuss and write about current natural resource options. What resources are abundant? Which are scarce? What conflicts are there over resources? How are resources conserved? How are they wasted? What are the consequences of wasted resources? What are examples of wasted resources from our own history? What are ways to conserve what we have? Students can consult the book, *50 Ways To Save The Planet*.

Options in an interpersonal conflict. Using some hypothetical interpersonal dilemmas, have students come up with all the possible options they can. If necessary, remind them of options like walking away, changing the subject, or saying something nice to the person who just insulted or hurt you. Then, as a group select the top two and worst two (as far as effectiveness in resolving the situation).

Using similar processes for generating interpretations and options. Choose a challenging ethical dilemma and ask students to (1) generate multiple interpretations of the situation, (2) evaluate the likelihood of the different interpretations (which ones are likely to be true and which ones are not likely to be true), and then (3) choose the most likely one. Next ask them to use the same processes to come up with the best option for action: (1) generate all the possibilities, (2) evaluate the likelihood of their success by identifying possible consequences, and then (3) select the best one.

Practice thinking outside the box. Here are websites to use for increasing skills in creative solving problem. Some have activities, others have information or quizzes. Try them all: http://minorkey.com/awlinks.html; http://www.jpb.com/index.html; http://www.ncdini.org/

Change your environment creatively. Have students identify one thing the class could do to enhance the classroom environment. After this is done, have students think about one thing they could do to enhance their environment at home.

Level 4: Integrate Knowledge and Procedures
Execute plans, Solve problems

Multiple interpretations and culture. Use an intercultural dilemma (from the Appendix) to have students predict how people from different cultures might interpret the same event. If there's time, discuss several dilemmas involving several different cultures and ask students to list the similarities and differences among the cultures (for example, similarities among some Western cultures like individualism and speaking one's mind bluntly—which isn't the case in many Latin or Asian cultures).

Interpreting Situations
by Responding Creatively

Ideas for Developing Skills

Level 4 (continued)

Sponsor a creative or invention fair. Invite local artists and inventors along with students of the school to present their creative expressions or inventions at an exhibition fair. Allow everyone time to prepare (several months).

Solve a community problem creatively. Use the steps suggested by Lewis and colleagues (1998) in *Kid's Guide to Social Action* (written for kids to use with worksheets and concrete guidelines): (1) Choose a problem in the neighborhood (Does an area feel unsafe? Smell bad? Look terrible? Are there needy people?). (2) Do your research (How do community members feel about the problem? What is the history of the problem?). (3) Brainstorm unusual, creative solutions and choose the one that seems most possible and will make the most difference. (4) Build coalitions of support. Find all the people that agree with you (neighborhood, community, city, state, businesses, agencies). (5) Figure out (with the help of your coalition) who is your opposition and work with them on overcoming their objections. (6) Advertise (send out a news release, call tv, radio, newspaper reporters, churches). (7) Raise money if you need to. (8) Carry out your solution. Make a list of the steps you need to take (e.g., write letters, give speeches, pass petitions). (9) Evaluate and reflect on whether the plan is working. Did you try everything, should you change something? Celebrate what you have done by writing about it, dramatizing it, drawing it. (10) Don't give up. Find the thing that will work.

Choose your own adventure. As group or individual projects, have students create "choose your own adventure" stories, in which there are several options for action at critical points in the story, followed by very different consequences. When a reader reads the story, he or she frequently gets to choose the next action and reads about the consequences (e.g., if you choose to do X, turn to page XX and see what happens; if you choose to do y, turn to page yy).

Surviving in other cultures. Have students generate many options for dealing with an unfamiliar situation or culture (not just other countries; include unfamiliar American subcultures like a ranch/farm, fast-paced business setting, artist colony).

Problem solving. Take a social problem and have students generate as many opinions as they can about how to solve it. Include opinions from different sectors of the community. For example, environmentalists, business owners, religious folk, artists, educators, parents, workers, professors, scientists, politicians.

Researching options for action. Choose an ethical dilemma that requires research to generate multiple interpretations of the situation and come up with possible options for resolution. Provide a few resources from which students can gather information that helps them generate multiple interpretations and ask them to be creative in coming up with options for resolution.

Respond Creatively

Essays. Students write persuasive essays on real or hypothetical conflicts, creatively coming up with alternative options.

Write an ending. Students write a choose-your-own adventure story with multiple action options and outcomes.

Individual performance.
Following a cooperative or class activity targeting a particular sensitivity skill, students are assessed on their individual performance using a new example.

Creative works. Have students create poems, songs, music, plays, and visual art. Or have students create new games or inventions.

Communications. Have students write reports, posters, public service announcements, or speeches.

ES-6 Interpreting Situations

Create a Climate
to Develop Skills in Interpreting Situations

Creativity Nurturance
- Give students choices to pursue their interests as class assignments.
- Provide opportunities for individual variability in how assignments are completed when possible.
- Provide opportunities for individual self-expression when possible.
- Encourage students to think of multiple options when solving problems—in every subject area.

Encourage Concern for Resources
- Model responsible uses of resources (e.g., don't be wasteful, only take what you need).
- Expect responsible resource use.
- Discuss resource use in particular fields of study.

Perceiving Morality
- Encourage students to take morality seriously.
- Remind students that virtually every action they take has consequences for someone else (and themselves).
- Keep drawing their attention to the little things they could do for each other and model them.

Sample Student Self-Monitoring
Interpreting Situations
Encourage active learning by having students learn to monitor their own learning

Determine what is happening
Can I describe (objectively) what I am observing?
How can I verify my observations and opinions?
I am aware of the different ways people think about this problem/situation.
I know where to get more information about this problem.

Perceive morality
I try to keep on my "moral toes."
I take morality seriously.
I try to have a positive effect on others.

Respond creatively
How do I interpret what I am observing?
What about me affects my interpretations?
How do other people interpret it differently?
What about them affects their interpretations?
Have I laid out every possible option?
Am I ignoring certain options for any reason?
I try new things.
I like to do things in different ways.

Ethical Sensitivity 7

Communicating Well

(Communicate well)

WHAT

Good communication involves skills in listening, speaking, writing, and non-verbal communication. The particular communication skills needed for an encounter can vary according to the social context of communication (one-on-one, small group, large group, peers, adults and authorities, strangers, younger children) and the cultural context (culture, male/female, school/work/home).

WHY

In order to be ethically sensitive, one must know how to communicate well (by speaking, writing, acting, listening, etc.). One must be able to get one's message across to those who might help or hinder the action. Not surprisingly, good communication skills are correlated with altruistic or helpful behavior.

**Communication
Mediums
to Practice**

Telling a story
Telling a joke
Conveying information
Brainstorming and being creative
Expressing a social-political
opinion as a citizen
Solving a problem
Giving directions

Web Wise
Test students and get information at http://discoveryhealth.queendom.com

Communicating Well

SUBSKILLS OVERVIEW

Subskill 1: Speak

When speaking pay attention to:
Eye contact
Body posture
Gestures
Congruent facial expressions
Voice tone, inflection, volume
Timing
Content of what is expressed (conciseness, clarity)
Effect on listener
Conveying emotion
Building camaraderie

For **Writing**, use current graduation standard conceptualizations. Pay attention to: *Clarity*, *conciseness*, *conveying emotion*, and *who is the reader*.

Subskill 2: Listen

When listening pay attention to:
Eye contact
Body posture
Conveying emotion
Nonverbal sounds

Subskill 3: Communicate nonverbally and alternatively

Body language
Design of environment: landscape, architecture, décor/environs, aesthetics
Clothing and grooming
Artistic expression: Fine art, dance, music, mime

Subskill 4: Monitor communication

Is my message getting across?
Am I clear and concise?
Do I know my audience?
How can I adjust after feedback?

**Communication Contexts
for Practice**

One-on-one
Small group of friends or peers
Large group of friend or peers
Individual strangers in public
Groups of strangers
With adults and authorities
With younger children

Communicating Well by Speaking and Listening

Speaking.
Martin Luther King, Jr., motivated his listeners through his oratorical speaking style. His "I have a dream" speech is one of the most famous of this century.

Listening.
Larry King, interviewer on CNN. Mr. King can talk to anyone, make anyone feel comfortable. He has great listening and empathy skills. He is very respectful of his guests.

Ideas for Developing Skills

Level 1: Immersion in Examples and Opportunities
Attend to the big picture, Learn to recognize basic patterns

Ways to listen and talk to one another. Students watch film or media clips from different cultural interactions and identify differences between those conversing in terms of posture, volume, eye contact, proximity. For example, (1) <u>How to take turns in conversation</u>: Turn-taking can vary by culture. Some cultures have longer pauses between turns, some have no pauses but use interruption as a means of changing turns. (2) <u>How to listen</u>: Listening protocol can vary by culture. In some cultures, the listener gazes at the speaker almost constantly, in other cultures hardly at all. In other cultures, the listener makes constant noises or nods the head as a sign support (but not necessarily understanding).

Clear expression in speaking. Students listen to or watch media clips and discuss whether or not the person expressed him or herself clearly, what they intended to express, how they might have done better, etc.

Building camaraderie. Identify methods (e.g., through media clips) that people use that make them easy to talk to (e.g., finding something in common, showing liking of the other person) and practice them.

What does listening mean? (1) The English word stems from two old English words: *hlystan*, which means 'hearing', and *hlosnian*, meaning 'to wait in suspense.' Discuss these facts. Search for evidence of good listening in a video or during class: rapt attention. (2) Listening means that you try to fully understand the perspective of the other person. One of the ways to do this is to ask a follow up question to make sure you understand what they mean.

Starred ⭐ activities within each subskill go together!

Communicating Well
by Speaking and Listening

Ideas for Developing Skills

Level 2: Attention to Facts and Skills
Focus on detail and prototypical examples, Build knowledge

Practice showing respect. How to show respect verbally and nonverbally in different situations (e.g., during academic debates in the classroom; at a church/temple/mosque, at a rock concert, at a classical music concert, in a museum, different cultural situations, etc.): (1) Discuss student experiences with these differences. (2) Students find out the codes or rules for appropriate communication from community members. They model these to classmates. Discuss. (3) Role play the ways to show respect verbally or non-verbally in these difference situations.

Practice effective speaking. Effective communication includes clear pronunciation, eye contact, completing one's sentences, and use of 'I-messages.' Demonstrate each of these techniques, and ask the students to identify what was effective about each example. **Assess:** Demonstrate one example in which you use poor eye contact. Use another example in which you do not complete your sentences. Use an example in which your thoughts are not organized effectively. Note whether the students identify which style is most effective and which are not and why they are not effective. Note whether the students correctly identified the type of ineffective communication in each example.

Practice expressing a feeling or idea. Practice different ways people express ideas and feelings in different contexts (e.g., how you get express enthusiasm one-on-one, small group, large audience). **Assess** with each student drawing a feeling or idea from a hat and having to act it out in front of the class or small group or partner; the group guesses what was being conveyed.

Practice showing empathy. Consider different ways to show empathy. (1) Discuss, model, and have students practice how to show empathy with different age groups and different cultures: (a) what to do when listening; (b) how to display understanding; (c) how to display sympathy or compassion. (2) Share experiences of emotional support and what it meant to the person. (3) Bring in the counselor (or other expert) to demonstrate empathy and listening skills.

Practice active listening. Discuss and have students practice Active Listening: (1) Use I-statements ('I feel___ when you ___ because ___'); (2) State feelings without attacking the other person; (3) Be assertive without being aggressive.

Listening to someone who is angry with you. Have students role play keeping their cool while someone yells at them. They should take their time answering, look for the underlying feeling beneath the anger. The angry person often feels (a) lonely, neglected, unloved, hurt or (b) afraid.

Starred activities within each subskill go together!

Communicating Well
by Speaking and Listening

Ideas for Developing Skills

 Communicating one-on-one. Discuss, model, and have students practice how to communicate effectively in dyads: (1) saying 'no' to peers gracefully; (2) how to be assertive when necessary; (3) nonverbal communication in particular situations.

Communication in a specific culture. Consider cultural differences in interpersonal communication. (1) Students learn from a partner or community member how to interact in that person's culture for a particular situation. They demonstrate the differences to the class. After everyone has presented (or after each presentation), the class discusses the differences. (2) Make a list of communication principles. Watch video clips or films of communication in different cultures and analyze differences in terms of your list of principles.

Saying no. Students role play an interaction with a friend who asks them to do something risky. Coached by classmates, students practice acting considerately but firmly, using appropriate language and effective nonverbal behavior.

Communicating to groups. Students practice giving an informative speech about a particular person or group of people (e.g., an admirable hero, an ethical leader, a group in need, a group suffering injustice).

Giving a speech. Have students give a speech to the class, and assess them on particular (practiced) communication skills, such as clear expression of their point, opening and closing statements, eye contact with the audience, interaction with the audience. **Assess** with typical rubrics for giving a speech (e.g., eye contact, organization, posture, tone, opening, conclusion, etc.).

Preparing for a stressful conversation (from Gibbs, Potter, & Goldstein, 1995). Discuss the steps for helping oneself deal with a stressful conversation: (1) Imagine yourself in the situation and how you will feel. (2) Who is responsible for the situation? (3) Imagine the other person in the situation and how they might feel. (4) Practice saying something in a calm, straightforward way. (5) Think about how the other person will feel and act in response to what you say. (6) If you anticipate the other person not reacting well, then think of something better to say. Practice these steps with different scenarios like: (a) asking a person out for a first date, (b) talking to the coach about an unfair decision, (c) speaking up against a bully for a victim, (d) telling a friend that you don't like them vandalizing school property (e.g., spray painting, destroying a book, carving into a desk or locker).

Starred activities within each subskill go together!

Communicating Well
by Speaking and Listening

Ideas for Developing Skills

Level 3 (continued)

Analyzing interactions. In journaling about a service-learning project, students discuss interactions with others, analyzing them for type of communication style.

Steps to good listening (from Forni, 2002, *Choosing Civility*). Discuss the steps to good listening and then practice them in role plays of everyday life.
1. <u>Plan your listening</u>: Tell yourself that you are listening now, give the speaker your full attention, and be silent.
2. <u>Show that you are listening</u>: Make eye contact, nod, interject small comments like "I understand," "right." Once in a while you may need to paraphrase what the person said just so you are sure you understood correctly.
3. <u>Be a cooperative listener</u>: Help the speaker reach a higher level of understanding by guiding their thinking aloud with the right open-ended questions (that don't intrude or are meant to satisfy your own curiosity).
4. <u>Assess what the speaker wants you to do</u>: Sometimes speakers want advice from the listener, but many times they do not.

Level 4: Integrate Knowledge and Procedures
Execute plans, Solve problems

Communicating under duress. Teacher or students put together a set of situations in which good and respectful communication is difficult (e.g., in a heated discussion about human rights it is difficult to keep communication open with people who take a different position). Discuss how to show respect and self-control. Role play these situations for students to practice maintaining good communication even when upset.

Communicating with diverse groups. (1) Students perform research (e.g., through reading and interviews) on how people in other cultures show they are listening and have empathy. Students find out what styles are appropriate when speaking to different people. Students or student groups demonstrate to the class. Assess student recall of what was presented in terms of how it was different from their culture. (2) During community projects or cross-age activities, ask students to self report and to rate each other on communication skills.

Ask community members to rate their student contacts. When a student behaves less than expected, have the student practice and return to the type of encounter to try communicating again.

Intercultural critical incidents. Discuss intercultural incidents in which miscommunication occurred (for example, use incidents and author discussion from *Cross-Cultural Dialogues*, Storti, 1994).

Personal interactions in community service. In journaling about a service learning project, students discuss interactions with others, analyzing them for type of communication style. Make sure they are aware of cultural difference for passive, assertive, aggressive styles.

Assessment Hints

Speak & Listen

 Tests. Use multiple-choice, true-false, short answer, or essay tests to assess student knowledge of specific speaking and listening skills.

Media clips. Use media clips or written scenarios and have students analyze and evaluate the speaking and listening behaviors presented either individually in writing or in small groups.

Role play. Have students role play and demonstrate specific speaking and listening skills.

Starred activities within each subskill go together!

ES-7 Communicating Well

Creative and Expert
Implementer
Real-Life Example

Communicating Well by Communicating Nonverbally and Alternatively

Mimes are artists who do not speak by show their emotions, ideas, and the space around them through gestures and body movements. They grab attention because they wear a white-face (indicating that they won't speak), dress in black and do not speak words but speak volumes nonverbally.

Ideas for Developing Skills

Level 1: Immersion in Examples and Opportunities
Attend to the big picture, Learn to recognize basic patterns

Communicating ideas and feelings nonverbally. Use media clips to discuss different ways people use to communicate the same idea or feeling in interactions with others.

Showing respect. Discuss media clips and whether interactions were respectful. Identify what was respectful and disrespectful in the interactions.

Showing empathy. Consider different ways to show empathy. (1) Discuss, model, and have students practice how to show empathy with different age groups and different cultures: (a) what to do when listening; (b) how to display understanding; (c) how to display sympathy or compassion. (2) Share experiences of emotional support and what it meant to the person. (3) Bring in a counselor (or other expert) to demonstrate empathy and listening skills. Assess by asking students to role play and exhibit skills.

Communicating ideas and feelings by the way one dresses: Identification. Examine different ways people communicate various feelings and ideas through their dress. Look at these within society and across societies.

Communicating ideas and feelings in room decor: Identification. Examine cultural differences in room design and decor. What ideas and feelings do different designs convey? How do environmental and societal constraints affect these designs?

Starred ✦ activities within each subskill go together!

Communicating Well by Communicating Nonverbally and Alternatively

Ideas for Developing Skills

Level 2: Attention to Facts and Skills
Focus on detail and prototypical examples, Build knowledge

Showing respect nonverbally. Modify activities in 'Showing Respect' in Speaking and Listening (p. 141) and address only nonverbals.

Showing empathy nonverbally. Modify activities in 'Showing Empathy' in Speaking and Listening (p. 141) and address only nonverbals.

Displaying assertive nonverbals. Discuss, model, and practice nonverbal communication that conveys passivity (e.g., victim-like: slouch, slower walking, fearful, no eye contact), aggression (victimizer-like: defiant, taking all the space, looking for eye contact), and assertive (calm but resolute walking, head up, purposeful).

Communicating ideas and feelings by the way one dresses: Interpretation. Examine different ways people communicate various feelings and ideas through their dress. Look at these within society and across societies.

Communicating ideas and feelings in room décor: Interpretation. Examine cultural differences in room design and décor. What ideas and feelings do different designs convey? How do environmental and societal constraints affect these designs?

Use the internet for activities. Get information for jigsaw learning at:
http://nonverbal.ucsc.edu/
Students can test their nonverbal communication skills at: http://nonverbal.ucsc.edu/

Level 3: Practice Procedures
Set goals, Plan steps of problem solving, Practice skills

Power of nonverbals. Students identify which nonverbals are most important to them for the different contexts in their lives. Then they go practice them appropriately and inappropriately in those contexts. Have them report on people's reactions.

Communicating ideas and feelings by the way one dresses: Creation. Examine different ways people communicate various feelings and ideas through their dress. Look at these within society and across societies. Using the techniques of the trade, students create their own dress design or outfits to convey a particular idea or feeling.

Starred activities within each subskill go together!

Communicating Well by Communicating Nonverbally and Alternatively

Ideas for Developing Skills

Starred ★ activities within each subskill go together!

Assessment Hints

Communicate Nonverbally and Alternatively

Media clips. Use media clips or written scenarios and have students analyze and evaluate the nonverbal communication behaviors presented either individually in writing or in small groups.

Role play. Have students role play and demonstrate specific nonverbal communication skills.

Level 3 (continued)

Communicating ideas and feelings in room décor: Creation.
Examine cultural differences in room design and décor. What ideas and feelings do different designs convey? How do environmental and societal constraints affect these designs? Using the techniques of the trade, students create their own room designs to convey a particular idea or feeling.

Level 4: Integrate Knowledge and Procedures
Execute plans, Solve problems

Only nonverbals. Sometimes, when you meet someone who speaks another language you don't know, you have to use nonverbals to communicate. Set up role plays for students to practice using nonverbals only to communicate (e.g., asking for directions to the movie theatre, asking for directions to McDonald's, etc.).

★**Communicating ideas and feelings by the way one dresses: Coaching.** Examine different ways people communicate various feelings and ideas through their dress. Look at these within society and across societies. Using the techniques of the trade, students coach others on using dress to convey a particular idea or feeling.

Communicating ideas and feelings in room décor: Coaching.
Examine cultural differences in room design and décor. What ideas and feelings do different designs convey? How do environmental and societal constraints affect these designs? Using the techniques of the trade, students coach others on using room decor to convey a particular idea or feeling.

Nonverbal cues that express warmth or coldness, as seen by mainstream U. S. culture
(based on Johnson, 1986, p. 163)

Nonverbal Cue	Cues that show warmth	Cues that show coldness
Tone of voice	Soft, gentle	Hard, rough, edgy
Facial expression	Smiling, attentive	Blank, frowning, aloof, tough
Posture	Relaxed, leaning forward	Tense, resistant, standing back
Eye contact	Looking in the eye, not staring	Looking away, not in the eye
Touching	Gentle, shoulder, arm	Avoiding touching, shrinking if touched
Gestures	Open, kind, firm handshake	Crossed arms, turned away
Spatial distance	Close	Far, stepping back
Movement	Mirroring, responsive	Stiff, non-responsive
Paralanguage (sounds)	Responsive use of mmm, etc.	Non-responsive

Communicating Well by Monitoring Communication

Advertisers and other people who sell products (for example, on television) use many techniques to get viewers interested in their products. As they try to tell a seductive story about the value of their products for a viewer's well-being, they use color, fashion, beauty, action, music, and other methods to get and keep our attention.

Creative and Expert Implementer Real-Life Example

Ideas for Developing Skills

Level 1: Immersion in Examples and Opportunities
Attend to the big picture, Learn to recognize basic patterns

Noticing success of communication. Use media clips of interactions in which speakers misunderstand each other and don't notice vs. interactions in which speakers misunderstand and try to rectify the misunderstanding. Discuss what the rectifiers are noticing. **Assess** with different media clips.

Noticing cultural differences. Invite people who are skilled multiculturally to speak to the class about how they make adjustments for different cultural audiences when they speak (one-on-one or with groups).

Level 2: Attention to Facts and Skills
Focus on detail and prototypical examples, Build knowledge

Using self-monitoring questions. Identify means one might use to determine if your listener understands what you are saying (e.g., non-verbal cues like eye contact or sounds, direct questioning, asking person to paraphrase, etc.). Find examples of people using these (media or real life). **Assess** with self-evaluation on a specified conversation.

Preparing for cultural differences. Have students gather information about how people from different cultures converse. Create a list of things to watch for. Have students practice these things in class.

Monitoring language for bias and prejudice. Use activities to help the students learn to monitor the language they use for bias and prejudice. The website for Teaching Tolerance (www.tolerance.org/teach/ has dozens of short and longer activities for doing this).

Communication skills test. Have students take the communications skills test at http://discoveryhealth.queendom.com. Use the questions for a discussion.

Starred ★ activities within each subskill go together!

Communicating Well by Monitoring Communication

Ideas for Developing Skills

Level 3: Practice Procedures
Set goals, Plan steps of problem solving, Practice skills

Self-monitoring skills. Practice self-monitoring of communication to others through role plays and coaching. **Assess** with a role play.

Cultural self-monitoring. Using ideas from interculturally skilled adults, have students monitor their own interactions with others who have different backgrounds. Use journals and structured questions.

Level 4: Integrate Knowledge and Procedures
Execute plans, Solve problems

New communication opportunities. Plan real-life communication opportunities for students that are unfamiliar. Have them record their success in communicating (or have a partner watch and evaluate).

New intercultural communication opportunities. Plan real-life communication opportunities for students that involve persons from another culture. Have them record their success in communicating (or have a partner watch and evaluate).

Assessment Hints

Monitor Communication

Speeches. Have students record their speeches using video or audio recorders. Students monitor their own communication by viewing/listening to their speeches.

Journaling. Have students journal on their practicing of speaking events.

Role play. Have students role play communication skills.

Sample Student Self-Monitoring
for Communicating Well

Encourage active learning by having students learn to monitor their own learning

Speak and Listen

I have good posture when speaking to a group.

My timing is working.

I am keeping eye contact.

I am paying attention to my nonverbal communication.

I am expressing myself clearly.

People understand me when I tell them my ideas.

I am practicing active listening.

I try to listen instead of thinking only of what I am going to say next.

People say I am a good listener.

Communicate Nonverbally and Alternatively

Am I looking for nonverbal cues to how people are reacting to me?

Am I moving my body in a way that is culturally offensive?

Am I moving assertively?

Monitor Communication

Is my message getting across?

Am I clear and concise?

Do I know my audience?

How can I adjust after feedback?

I watch other people to understand their reactions to my ideas.

Am I a successful communicator in the following contexts?

One-on-one

Small group of friends or peers

Large group of friend or peers

Individual strangers in public

Groups of strangers

With adults and authorities

With younger children

Am I practicing the following types of communication?

Telling a story

Telling a joke

Conveying information

Giving directions

Solving a problem

Brainstorming and being creative

Expressing a social-political opinion as a citizen

Create a Climate
to Develop Communication Skills

Generally:

- Emphasize the importance of good human communication (e.g., that poor communication is frustrating for all, doesn't get your needs met, etc.).
- Emphasize that learning to be a good communicator takes practice.Encourage self-expression and the continual focus on the improvement of skills.
- Encourage good communication among the students in the classroom. Stop activities to work out a conflict between students.
- Point out that different cultures may have different styles and explore these styles with the students.

Selections to Post in the Classroom
for Communicating Well

Communication virtues
for a respectful, multicultural classroom
(Gollnick & Chin, 1994, 314-315)

Tolerance, patience, and respect for differences

The willingness to listen

The inclination to admit that one may be mistaken

The ability to reinterpret or translate one's own concerns in a way that
makes them comprehensible to others

Self-imposition of restraint in order that others may have a turn to speak

A disposition to express oneself honestly and sincerely

Ethical Sensitivity Appendix

Lesson Planning Guide

'Linking to the Community' Worksheet

Rubric Examples
>   Journaling
>   Papers or Reports
>   Group Project
>   Student Interactions

Special Activities
>   Cognitive Apprenticeship
>   Cooperative Learning
>   Guidelines for Cross-Age Tutoring
>   Reciprocal Teaching
>   Intercultural Dilemmas
>   Interpersonal Dilemmas
>   Tolerance Survey
>   The Jigsaw Method
>   Structured Controversy

Making a Strategic Plan for Change

Linking ES Skills to Search Institute Assets

Recommended Resources for Character Education

Resources/References for Ethical Sensitivity

Lesson Planning Guide

1. **Select an ethical category and identify the subskill you will address in your lesson(s).**

2. **Select a graduation standard or academic requirement and identify the sub-components.**

3. **Match up the ethical sub-skill with the academic sub-components.**

4. **Generate lesson activities using these elements:**

   (a) Enlist the communities resources.
   (For ideas, consult the Linking to Community worksheet, pp. 154-159.)

   (b) Focus on a variety of teaching styles and intelligences.
   Teaching styles: Visual, Auditory, Tactile, Kinesthetic, Oral, Individual/Cooperative, Olfactory, Gustatory, Spatial

   Intelligences: Musical, Bodily-Kinesthetic, Spatial Logico-Mathematical, Linguistic, Interpersonal, Intrapersonal

   (c) Identify questions that you can ask that promote different kinds of thinking and memory.

   Creative Thinking

   Prospective Thinking

   Retrospective Thinking

   Motivational Thinking

   Practical Thinking

   Types of Memory:

   > Autobiographical (personal experience)

   > Narrative (storyline)

   > Procedural (how to)

   > Semantic (what)

5. **Create an activity for each <u>level of expertise</u> you will address (worksheet provided on next page). Indicate which activities fit with which lesson. For each activity, indicate how you will <u>assess learning</u>.**

Lesson Planning Guide
(continued)

ACTIVITY   STUDENT ASSESSMENT

Level 1: Immersion in Examples and Opportunities
(Attend to the big picture, Learn to recognize basic patterns)

Level 2: Attention to Facts and Skills
(Focus on detail and prototypical examples, Build knowledge)

Level 3: Practice Procedures
(Set goals, Plan steps of problem solving, Practice skills)

Level 4: Integrate Knowledge and Procedures
(Execute plans, Solve problems)

Ethical Sensitivity Appendix

CHECKLIST FOR
Linking to the Community

What resources must be accessed for learning the skill or subskill?

What resources must be identified to successfully complete the skill or subskill?

1. SOCIAL NETWORK RESOURCES

Circle the resources that must be accessed for learning the skill:

Family_____   Friendship_____   Service group_____

Neighborhood_____   Social groups _____   Community_____

City_____   Park & Rec_____   State_____

National _____   International_____

Other:_____Other:_____

On the line next to each circled item, indicate the <u>manner of contact</u>:

Contact in person (P), by telephone (T)

2. SEMANTIC KNOWLEDGE RESOURCES

Circle the resources that must be accessed for learning the skill:

Books and other library sources_____   Web_____

Librarians_____   Educators and Intellectuals_____

Business leaders_____   Community experts_____

Other:_____   Other:_____

On the line next to each circled item, indicate the <u>manner of contact</u>:

Contact in person (P), Email (E), Web (W), Letter (L), Telephone (T)

CHECKLIST FOR
Linking to the Community
(continued)

3. AUTHORITY STRUCTURE RESOURCES

Circle the resources that must be accessed for learning the skill:

School officials____   Government officials (all levels) ____ United Nations____

Other Leaders:_____

_____

_____

Indicate the manner of contact for each item:

Contact in person (P), Telephone (T), Letter (L), Email (E)

4. ORGANIZATIONAL RESOURCES

What types of organizations can give guidance?

_____

_____

_____

_____

How can they help?

_____

_____

_____

_____

_____

_____

_____

_____

Ethical Sensitivity Appendix

Ethical Sensitivity Appendix

5. AGE GROUP RESOURCES

Circle the resources that must be accessed for learning the skill:

- Teen groups in various community organizations_____

    Specify:

- School groups_____

    Specify:

- Senior citizen groups_____

    Specify:

- Children's groups_____

    Specify:

- Women's groups_____

    Specify:

- Men's groups_____

    Specify:

Indicate the manner of contact for each circled item:

Contact in person (P), Telephone (T), Letter (L), Email (E)

CHECKLIST FOR
Linking to the Community
(continued)

6. MATERIAL RESOURCES

<u>Types of Materials</u>

* scraps (from scrap yards)

* second-hand (from second-hand stores, recycling places)

* new

* handmade

Identify the resources that must be accessed for learning the skill:

What materials do you need for your project?

_____

_____

_____

Where can you get it?

_____

_____

_____

How can you get it?

_____

_____

_____

Indicate the manner of contact for each item:

Contact in person (P), Telephone (T), Letter (L), Email (E)

Ethical Sensitivity Appendix

CHECKLIST FOR
Linking to the Community
(continued)

7. **EXPERTISE RESOURCES**

Types of Expertise

social networking _____   design_____   musical _____

physical (game/sport, dance) _____ creating_____ knowledge _____

finance_____   selling _____

Identify the resources that must be accessed for learning the skill:

What expertise is required?

_____

_____

_____

_____

Who has expertise?

_____

_____

_____

Can I develop expertise or must I depend on an expert?

_____

_____

Who can help me figure out what to do?

_____

_____

_____

Indicate the manner of contact for each item:

Telephone (T), Take a class (C), Contact in person (P), Book (B)

CHECKLIST FOR
Linking to the Community
(continued)

8. FINANCIAL RESOURCES

Circle the sources that must be accessed for learning the skill:

Grants___   Loans___   Donors___

Earn money___

Bartering (use library and experts to find these out) ___

Indicate the manner of contact for each circled item:

Contact in person (P), Telephone (T), Letter (L), Email (E)

9. PERSONAL RESOURCES

What abilities and skills do I have that I can use to reach the goal?

_____

_____

_____

_____

10. OTHER RESOURCES

What other resources might be needed or are optional?

_____

_____

_____

_____

Ethical Sensitivity Appendix

Rubric Examples

GUIDES FOR CREATING YOUR OWN RUBRIC

Creating Rubrics
(Blueprint of behavior for peak or acceptable level of performance)

❖ Establish Learner Outcome goals
❖ Cluster these characteristics
❖ Determine which combinations of characteristics show
      Unsatisfactory, Satisfactory, Excellent 'job'
❖ Create examples of work showing different levels of performance
❖ List expectations on a form
❖ Present criteria to students ahead of time

RUBRIC FOR JOURNALING

Quality of Journaling		
Content: Quantity Few requirements for content are covered. 0 1 2 3	Most requirements are included fairly well. 4 5 6 7	Content requirements are thoroughly covered. 8 9 10
Content: Type Rarely are both feelings and thoughts included in entries. 0 1 2 3	Sometimes both feelings and thoughts are included in entries. 4 5 6 7	Both feelings and thoughts are included in entries. 8 9 10
Content: Clarity Entries are difficult to understand. 0 1 2 3	Entries can be understood with some effort. 4 5 6 7	Entries are easily understood. 8 9 10

Rubric Examples (continued)

RUBRIC FOR PAPERS OR REPORTS

Qualities of Paper or Written Report		
Organization The paper is difficult to follow. 0 1 2 3	The paper is easy to follow and read. 4 5 6 7	All relationships among ideas are clearly expressed by the sentence structures and word choices. 8 9 10
Writing Style The style of the writing is sloppy, has no clear direction, looks like it was written by several people. 0 1 2 3	The format is appropriate with correct spelling, good grammar, good punctuation and appropriate transition sentences. 4 5 6 7	The paper is well written and is appropriate for presentation in the firm. 8 9 10
Content The paper has no point. The ideas are aimless, disconnected. 0 1 2 3	The paper makes a couple of clear points but weakly, with few supportive facts. 4 5 6 7	The paper makes one or two strong points. Support for these arguments is well described. 8 9 10

Rubric Examples (continued)

RUBRIC FOR GROUP PROJECT
(Bloomer & Lutz as cited in Walvoord & Anderson, 1998)

Ethical Sensitivity Appendix

Evaluation of a Group Project*	Rating
Comprehension: Seemed to understand requirements for assignment.	0 1 2 3 Not Observed
Problem Identification and Solution: Participated in identifying and defining problems and working towards a solution.	0 1 2 3 Not Observed
Organization: Approached tasks (such as time management) in systematic way.	0 1 2 3 Not Observed
Acceptance of responsibility: Took responsibility for assigned tasks in the project.	0 1 2 3 Not Observed
Initiative/motivation: Made suggestions, sought feedback, showed interest in group decision making and planning.	0 1 2 3 Not Observed
Creativity: Considered ideas from unusual or different viewpoints.	0 1 2 3 Not Observed
Task completion: Followed through in completing own contributions to the group project.	0 1 2 3 Not Observed
Attendance: Attended planning sessions, was prompt and participated in decision making.	0 1 2 3 Not Observed

Add Total Score

Total:_____

Divide by number of items scored with a number

Average:_____

Comments:

Rubric Examples (continued)

RUBRIC FOR STUDENT INTERACTIONS
(Bloomer & Lutz as cited in Walvoord & Anderson, 1998)

Project-related Interactions with others*	Rating
Collaboration: Worked cooperatively with others.	0 1 2 3 Not Observed
Participation: Contributed a 'fair share' to group project, given the nature of individual assignment	0 1 2 3 Not Observed
Attitude: Displayed positive approach and made constructive comments in working toward goal.	0 1 2 3 Not Observed
Independence: Carried out tasks without overly depending on other group members	0 1 2 3 Not Observed
Communication: Expressed thoughts clearly.	0 1 2 3 Not Observed
Responsiveness: Reacted sensitively to verbal and nonverbal cues of other group members.	0 1 2 3 Not Observed

Add Total Score   Total:_____

Divide by number of items scored with a number   Average:_____

Comments:

Ethical Sensitivity Appendix

Special Activities

COGNITIVE APPRENTICESHIP
(Collins, Hawkins, & Carver, 1991, p. 228)

Teach *process* (how to) and *provide guided experience* in cognitive skills.

Teach *content* relevant to the task.

Teach this content for each subject area:

 Strategic knowledge: how to work successfully in the subject area

 Domain knowledge: the kind of knowledge experts know

 Problem solving strategies particular to the subject area

Learning strategies for the subject area

Teaching methods to use:

 Expert modeling

 Coaching

 Scaffolding (lots of structured assistance at first, gradual withdrawal of support)

 Articulation by students

 Reflection

 Exploration

How to sequence material:

 Increasing complexity

 Increasing diversity

 Global (the big picture) before the local (the detail)

Learning environment should emphasize:

 Situated learning

 Community of practice

 Intrinsic motivation

 Cooperation

COOPERATIVE LEARNING

Necessary elements in using cooperative learning to improve role-taking (Bridgeman, 1981)

1. Required interdependence and social reciprocity
2. Consistent opportunity to be an expert
3. Integration of varied perspectives and appreciation for the result
4. Equal status cooperation
5. Highly structured to allow easy replication of these interactions

Special Activities

GUILDELINES FOR CROSS-GRADE TUTORING

(Heath & Mangiola, 1991)

1. Allow a preparation period of at least 1 month to 6 weeks for the student tutors.

2. Use as much writing as possible in the context of the tutoring from the very beginning. Use a variety of sources and use the tutoring as a basis for tutors to write to different audiences.

3. Make field notes meaningful as a basis for conversation by providing students with occasions to share their notes orally.

4. Provide students with supportive models of open-ended questioning.

5. Emphasize the ways in which tutors can extend tutees' responses and elicit elaboration from tutees in order to impress upon them the importance of talk in learning.

6. Discuss the ways the topic relates to students' experiences.

7. Provide opportunities for tutors to prepare.

8. Develop real audiences for the students' work.

RECIPROCAL TEACHING (RT)

Context	One-on-one in laboratory settings	Groups in resource rooms	Naturally occurring groups in classrooms	Work groups fully integrated into science classrooms
Activities	Summarizing, questioning, clarifying, predicting	Gist and analogy	Complex argument structure	Thought experiments
Materials	Unconnected passages	Coherent content	Research-related resources material	Student-prepared
Pattern of use	Individual strategy training	Group discussion	Planned RT for learning content and jigsaw teaching	Opportunistic use of RT

Ethical Sensitivity Appendix

Special Activities

INTERCULTURAL DILEMMAS

Also see *Cross-Cultural Dialogues: 74 Brief Encounters with Cultural Difference* (Storti, 1994) and *Developing Intercultural Awareness: A Cross-Cultural Training Handbook* (Kohls & Knight, 1999).

To stretch students' perspective taking abilities and sensitivity to alternative viewpoints, educators often use intercultural dilemmas as a source for discussion. Cultural misunderstandings often occur because of different viewpoints regarding conflict, how to show respect, and what is appropriate social behavior. Here are a few dilemmas that can be used for discussion.

DIRECTIONS: After reading the scenario one or more times, ask students to explain the differing viewpoints apparent in the scenario. Students identify possible reasons a person behaves in a particular way—what value differences are on display?

The Concert

Erin is a 14-year-old American high school student spending a month in Mexico as part of an exchange program. She lives with a Mexican family and has become good friends with their 13-year-old daughter, Rosa. She has also gotten to know Rosa's other friends. Erin likes all the new things about life in Mexico but feels frustrated that there are more rules. She misses freedoms from home like playing outside and shopping at the corner store whenever she wants to. Her new friends prefer to just stay home or at each other's houses. Whenever Erin suggests to her friends that they do something new, the others seem very quiet and don't want to talk about it. She was very excited when she heard that one of her favorite music groups was going to be coming to town so she suggested to Rosa and her friends that they should all go. Although the girls admitted they would like to go, they looked very nervous and said they didn't think they could. Erin kept trying to bring it up over the next few days, but someone always changed the subject.

Missing the Newspaper Meeting

Mariko was a new exchange student from Japan at a middle school in Minnesota. She was a little nervous at first, but she found herself becoming familiar with the routines and lifestyle. She had also become friends with a girl named Linda, who sometimes gave her a ride to school. One morning, on the way to school, Linda asked Mariko if she would like to help out with the school newspaper, for which Linda was a junior editor. Mariko replied hesitantly that she didn't think her English was good enough and that it would be better to ask someone else. Linda told Mariko that her English skills would be just fine and that she'd look for her after school to show her where the newspaper staff meets. That afternoon, Mariko didn't show up, even though Linda looked for her for at least an hour. The next time she saw Mariko, Linda asked what had happened to her. Mariko apologized and said she'd had to study for an exam and she didn't really feel she was capable of doing the work. Linda was exasperated. "Well, why didn't you just say so?" she demanded of Mariko. Mariko just looked down and said nothing.

Special Activities

INTERPERSONAL DILEMMAS

To stretch students' perspective taking abilities and sensitivity to alternative viewpoints, educators often use social dilemmas as a source for discussion. Here are interpersonal dilemmas that can be used to increase sensitivity to others.

<u>DIRECTIONS</u>: After reading the scenario one or more times, first ask students to explain the different viewpoints. Then ask students to think of possible ways to remedy the situation. How can you act sensitively? How could you behave more sensitively in the future?

The Ridiculous Hat

You're eating and hanging out with some of your friends at the tables outside a fast food restaurant. This guy walks up and you recognize him as a new student who is playing on your soccer team. As he comes closer, you all notice that he is wearing a strange cap on his head. When you realize that you and all of your friends are staring at him, you try to break the tension by calling out, "Hey! Nice hat." Everyone in your group laughs, and you smile at him, expecting him to smile back. Instead, he looks very embarrassed and rushes inside the restaurant. When he comes back out, he doesn't even look up. He walks off without saying anything, still looking a bit embarrassed.

Cutting the Line

You have been waiting in the movie ticket line with a friend for about 10 minutes out in the cold and the line seems to be moving slowly. You start to wonder if the show you wanted to see might sell out. As you lean forward to check what time the movie starts, two girls run up to the lady in front of you and hug her excitedly. The three start chattering away and laughing and several people behind you seem annoyed that they've cut into the line.

A Person Without a Home

You decide to take a weekend job volunteering at the public library. After you have been working there a few weeks, you notice a woman who comes in almost every day and sits down with a stack of books. She doesn't leave until the library closes in the evening. One day your boss jokes with her about how she "lives at the library," and is surprised to find out that she is actually homeless. The whole library staff is surprised because she is not what you would expect a homeless person to be.

The Boy at the Bus Stop

You are waiting at the bus stop early in the morning. You have a lot on your mind because you have a busy day ahead of you. Out of the corner of your eye, you see a boy, several years younger than you, looking around anxiously. He looks like he's in a hurry and he can't decide where to go. He glances in your direction for a moment and looks like he is about to say something. He opens his mouth to speak but stops suddenly just as he gets close enough to say something. He leaves quickly.

Special Activities

TOLERANCE SURVEY

- Please circle the number that shows how fairly you think the teacher treats the following people:

	Very fair	Fair enough	Not fair at all
boys	1	2	3
girls	1	2	3
students of a different race	1	2	3
students from another culture	1	2	3
students with disabilities	1	2	3
students with a different religion	1	2	3
students who are overweight	1	2	3
students who look different	1	2	3

- Please circle the number that show how fairly you think students in our class treat the following people:

	Very fair	Fair enough	Not fair at all
boys	1	2	3
girls	1	2	3
students of a different race	1	2	3
students from another culture	1	2	3
students with disabilities	1	2	3
students with a different religion	1	2	3
students who are overweight	1	2	3
students who look different	1	2	3

- Do you think you've ever been embarrassed or treated unfairly for being different? _____yes _____no

If you said yes, look at the following list of ways that people can be different and then check the ones that you feel have made others treat you unfairly.

I have been embarrassed or treated unfairly because I am _____.

_____a girl	_____a different race
_____a boy	_____from a different culture
_____a person with a disability	_____different in physical appearance (weight, acne, height)
_____a particular religion	_____other

- Sometimes people are unfair to others by bullying or teasing, but other times they hurt them just as much by ignoring them. Please check which types of people have been ignored or teased in our class.

Ignoring	Bullying/Teasing	
_____	_____	students from other cultures
_____	_____	students of a different race
_____	_____	students with a different religion
_____	_____	students with disabilities
_____	_____	students who look different
_____	_____	students students who are overweight
_____	_____	students who are very short or tall

In your opinion, what are the worst social problems in our class?

_____

What would you do to improve social problems in our class?

_____

- Circle which one you are: Girl   Boy

Special Activities

THE JIGSAW METHOD
(For more information, see Aronson & Patnoe, 1997, *The Jigsaw Classroom*)

The Jigsaw Method of cooperative learning helps children work together on an equal basis. It has been shown to improve empathy for fellow students, mastery of course material, liking of school and liking of classmates.

<u>Goal:</u> That students treat each other as resources
<u>Instructional outcome:</u> Students learn that it is possible to work together without sacrificing excellence.
<u>Structure:</u>

> Individual competition is incompatible with success.
> Success is dependent on cooperative behavior.
> All students has unique information to bring to the group.

You must provide material written by relative experts. This could be an article broken into pieces or could be cards on which you write critical information.

1. Divide the written material into 3-6 coherent parts (could be by paragraphs).
2. Assign students to 3-5 groups.
3. Assign one part of the material to each group member.
4. Those with the same part meet in groups to learn their knowledge (10-15 minutes).
5. Group members return to their original groups to learn from their group.
6. Everyone takes a quiz on all the material.

STRUCTURED CONTROVERSY

The steps for a structured academic controversy (Johnson & Johnson, 1997) are as follows:

(1) Select an issue relevant to what you are studying. Select two or more opinions on the issue.

(2) Form advocacy teams by putting the students into groups for each different opinion. Either put together a list of supporting statements for each opinion, or have students research the opinion and come up with their own supporting statements (if this is done, provide guidance and feedback for the accuracy and comprehensiveness of the supporting statements they generate). Each group prepares a persuasive statement based on the supporting statements of their opinion.

(3) Have each group present its persuasive case to the other groups without interruption. Students in the listening groups should listen carefully and take notes to learn the other opinion well.

(4) Have open discussion among the groups with advocacy of their own position and refutation of other positions (respectfully).

(5) Groups trade positions on the issue to take another group's perspective. The group must present the other perspective to the others as sincerely and persuasively as the original group did. The group can add new facts, information, or arguments to the position (based on what they have already learned) to make it more persuasive.

(6) All individuals drop their advocacy and group-orientation to discuss the positions again and try to come to a consensus about which position is the best. The position can be one that is a synthesis of two or more, as long as the position isn't a simple compromise.

Ethical Sensitivity Appendix

Special Activities

STRUCTURED CONTROVERSY
LESSON PLANNING SHEET

Grade Level_____   Subject area_____

Size of group_____   How groups formed_____

Room arrangement_____

Issue_____

    One perspective_____

    Second perspective_____

    Third perspective_____

Student materials required_____

Define the controversy_____

_____

_____

Making a strategic plan for change

1. **What I/we want to change:**

2. **The end result I/we want:**

3. **What is current reality—now?** Identify the difference between where things stand now and where you want to get to.

4. **What steps do I/we need to take to get to the desired end result?** Brainstorm on methods or strategies to reach your objectives. Don't eliminate any methods or strategies at this point.

5. **How will I/we know my/our actions are working?** Brainstorm on ways to check that actions are or are not working.

6. **Now select the best goals and the best set of steps to reach them.** Make sure:
- That the goals are going to reach the end result we desire. (Imagine the strategies successfully completed.)
- To quantify the goal where you can.
- To translate comparative terms (e.g., more, better, less, increased) into their actual goals.
- To create long-term, lasting results rather than just solving individual problems.
- That your goals describe an actual result rather than only a process for achieving that result.
- That your goals are specific.

Linking ES Skills to Search Institute Assets

VIRTUE / SUBSKILL	ES-1 Emotion	ES-2 Taking Persectives	ES-3 Connecting to Others	ES-4 Diversity	ES-5 Controlling Social Bias	ES-6 Interpret Situations	ES-7 Communic-ating Well
1. Family support							
2. Positive family comm.		*					*
3. Other adult relationships		*					
4. Caring neighborhood							
5. Caring school climate							
6. Parent involvement in school		*					
7. Community values youth							
8. Youth as resources						*	
9. Service to others				*	*		
10. Safety							
11. Family boundaries		*					
12. School boundaries		*					
13. Neighborhood boundaries		*					
14. Adult role models		*		*	*		
15. Positive peer influence				*			
16. High expectations							
17. Creative activities							
18. Youth programs							
19. Religious community							
20. Time at home							
21. Achievement motivation							
22. School engagement						*	
23. Homework							
24. Bonding to school		*		*			
25. Reading for pleasure							
26. Caring		*		*	*		
27. Equality and social justice	*	*		*	*		
28. Integrity				*	*		
29. Honesty		*		*	*		
30. Responsibility		*		*	*		
31. Restraint				*	*	*	
32. Planning and decision making	*	*	*	*	*	*	*
33. Interpersonal competence		*					*
34. Cultural competence		*		*	*		*
35. Resistance skills				*	*		*
36. Peaceful conflict resolution							
37. Personal power							
38. Self-esteem							
39. Sense of purpose		*					
40. Positive view of personal future							

Recommended Resources for Character Education

De Vries, R., & Zan, B. S. (1994). *Moral classrooms, moral children: Creating a constructivist atmosphere in early education.* New York: Teachers College Press.

Elias, M. J., Arnold, H., & Hussey, C. S. (Eds.). (2002). *EQ + IQ = Best leadership practices for caring and successful schools.* Thousand Oaks, CA: Corwin Press

Gootman, M. E. (2008). *The caring teacher's guide to discipline: Helping students learn self-control, responsibility, and respect, K-6* (3rd ed.). Thousand Oaks, CA: Corwin Press.

Greene, A. (1996). *Rights to responsibility: Multiple approaches to developing character and community.* Tucson, AZ: Zephyr.

Jweid, R., & Rizzo, M. (2001). *Building character through literature: A guide for middle school readers.* Lanham, MD: Scarecrow.

Kirschenbaum, H. (1994). *100 ways to enhance values and morality in schools and youth meetings.* Boston: Allyn & Bacon.

Lantieri, L., & Goleman, D. (2008). *Building emotional intelligence: Techniques to cultivate inner strength in children.* Boulder, CO: Sounds True, Incorporated.

Liebling, C. R. (1986). *Inside view and character plans in original stories and their basal reader adaptations.* Washington, DC: National Institute of Education.

Miller, J. C., & Clarke, C. (1998). *10-minute life lessons for kids: 52 fun and simple games and activities to teach your child trust, honesty, love, and other important values.* New York: HarperPerennial Library.

Nucci, L. P., & Narvaez, D. (Eds.). (2008). *Handbook of moral and character education.* New York: Routledge.

Power, F. C., Nuzzi, R. J., Narvaez, D., Lapsley, D. K., & Hunt, T. C. (Eds.). (2008). *Moral education: A handbook* (Vols. 1-2). Westport, CT: Praeger.

Ryan, K., & Bohlin, K. E. (2000). *Building character in schools: Practical ways to bring moral instruction to life.* San Francisco: Jossey-Bass.

Ryan, K., & Wynne, E. A. (1996). *Reclaiming our schools: Teaching character, academics, and discipline.* Upper Saddle River, NJ: Prentice Hall.

Watson, M., & Eckert, L. (2003). *Learning to trust.* San Francisco: Jossey-Bass.

Ethical Sensitivity Appendix

Resources/References for Ethical Sensitivity

Adedjouma, D. (1996). *The palm of my heart: Poetry by African-American children*. New York: Lee & Low.

Archambault, R. (1964). (Ed.). *John Dewey on education*. New York: Random House.

Aronson, E., & Patnoe, S. (1997). *The jigsaw classroom: Building cooperation in the classroom*. New York: Longman.

Banks, S. H., & Saflund, B. (1993). *Remember my name*. New York: Scholastic.

Begun, R.W. (1995). *Ready-to-use social skills & activities*. New York: Center for Applied Research in Education.

Bridgeman, D. (1981). Enhanced role-taking through cooperative interdependence: A field study. *Child Development, 52*, 1231-1238.

Byars, B. D. (1985). *Cracker Jackson*. New York: Viking Kestrel.

Byrnes, D. A., & Kiger, G. (1996). *Common bonds: Anti-bias teaching in a diverse society*. New York: Association for Childhood Education.

Colby, A., & Damon, W. (1992). *Some do care: Contemporary lives of moral commitment*. New York: Free Press.

Collins, A., Hawkins, J., & Carver. S. (1991). *A cognitive apprenticeship for disadvantaged students*. Washington, DC: U.S. Department of Education.

Combs, A. (1962). *Perceiving, behaving, becoming: A new focus for education*. Washington, DC: Association for Supervision and Curriculum Development.

Crick, N., & Dodge, K. (1994). A review and reformulation of social information processing in children's social adjustment. *Psychological Bulletin, 115*, 74-101.

Cushman, K. (1994). *Catherine, called Birdy*. New York: Clarion Books.

Cushman, K. (1995). *The midwife's apprentice*. New York: Clarion Books.

Davis, O. (1978). *Escape to freedom: A play about young Frederick Douglass*. New York: Viking Press.

Diamond, B. J., & Moore, M. A. (1995). *Multicultural literacy: Mirroring the new reality of the classroom*. New York: Longman.

Duncan, C. (1999). *Worlds apart: Why poverty exists in rural America*. New Haven, CT: Yale University Press.

Ehman, L. H. (1980). The American school in the political socialization process. *Review of Educational Research, 50*(1), 99-102.

Ehrenreich, B. (2001). *Nickled and dimed: On (not) getting by in America*. New York: Metropolitan Books.

Eisenberg, N., & Mussen, P. (1989). *The roots of prosocial behavior in children*. New York: Cambridge University Press.

Estes, E. (1990). *The hundred dresses. Innovations, experiencing literature in the classroom*. Jefferson City, MO: Scholastic.

Forni, P. (2002). *Choosing civility: The twenty-five rules of considerate conduct*. New York: St. Martins Press.

Fowler, S. M., & Mumford, M. G. (1995). *Intercultural sourcebook: Cross-cultural training methods*. New York: Intercultural Press.

Fox, P. (1984). *One-eyed cat: A novel*. Scarsdale, NY: Bradbury Press.

Fox, P., & Keith, E. (1973). *The slave dancer: A novel*. Scarsdale, NY: Bradbury Press.

Friel, J., & Friel, L. (2000). *The seven best things smart teens do*. Deerfield Beach, FL: Health Communications.

Fritz, J. (1995). *You want women to vote, Lizzie Stanton?* New York: Putnam.

George, J. (1990). *On the far side of the mountain*. New York: Dutton Children's Books.

Gibbs, J., Potter, G., & Goldstein, A. (1995). *The EQUIP program: Teaching youth to think and act responsibly through a peer-helping approach*. Champaign, IL: Research Press.

Gollnick, D., & Chinn, P. (1994). *Multicultural education in a pluralistic society*. Columbus, OH: Merrill.

Grant, C., & Sleeter, C. (1998). *Turning on learning*. Upper Saddle River, NJ: Merrill.

Hahn, T. N. (1988). *The heart of understanding*. Berkeley, CA: Parallax.

Heath, S., & Mangiola, L. (1991). *Children of promise: Literate activity in linguistically and culturally diverse classrooms*. Washington, DC: National Education Association.

Hendricks, G., & Wills, R. (1975). *The centering book*. New York: Prentice-Hall.

Jackson, S. (1980). *The lottery.* Cambridge, MA: R. Bentley.

Johnson, D. (1986). *Reaching out: Interpersonal effectiveness and self-actualization* (3rd ed.). Englewood Cliffs, NJ: Prentice-Hall.

Johnson, D. W., & Johnson, F. (1997). *Joining together: Group theory and group skills* (6th ed.). Boston: Allyn & Bacon.

Kabagarama, D. (1997). *Breaking the ice: A guide to understanding people from other cultures* (2nd ed.). New York: Prentice Hall.

King, C., & Osborne, L. (1997). *Oh freedom!: Kids talk about the Civil Rights movement with people who made it happen.* New York: A. A. Knopf.

Kohls, R., & Knight, J. (1999). *Developing intercultural awareness: A cross-cultural training handbook* (2nd ed.). Yarmouth, ME: Intercultural Press.

Ladson-Billings, G. (1991). *The dreamkeepers: Successful teachers of African-American children.* New York: Jossey-Bass.

Ledoux, J. (1996). *The emotional brain.* New York: Simon and Schuster.

Lewis, B. A., Espeland, P., & Pernu, C. (1998). *The kid's guide to social action: How to solve the social problems you choose and turn creative thinking into positive action.* Minneapolis, MN: Freespirit.

Levine, S. (1990). *Save our planet: 52 things kids can do.* New York: John Wiley & Sons.

Lickona, T. (1992). *Educating for character: How our schools can teach respect and responsibility.* New York: Bantam.

Loeb, P.R. (1999). *Soul of a citizen.* New York: St. Martin's Griffin.

Mandela, N. (1996). *Mandela: An illustrated autobiography.* Boston: Little, Brown.

McKissack, P., & McKissack, F. (1994). *Black diamond: The story of the negro baseball leagues.* New York: Scholastic.

Mills, L. A. (1991). *The rag coat.* Boston: Little, Brown.

Morris, J. (1994). *The Harvey girls: The women who civilized the west.* New York: Walker & Co.

Narvaez, D. (1996, April). *Moral perception: A new construct?* Paper presented at the annual meeting of the American Educational Research Association, New York.

Novaco, R. (1975). *Anger control.* Lexington, MA: D.C. Heath.

O'Dell, S. (1970). *Sing down the moon.* Boston: Houghton Mifflin.

Ontario Ministry of Education. (1991). *Unity in diversity: A curriculum resource guide for ethno-cultural equity and anti-racism education.* Toronto, Ontario: Author.

Paterson, K. (1988). *Park's quest.* New York: Lodestar Books.

Paul, R. (1987). *Critical thinking handbook, 4-6th grades: A guide for remodeling lesson plans in language arts, social studies, and science.* Rohnert Park, CA: Foundation Critical Thinking, Sonoma State University.

Philbrick, W. R. (1993). *Freak the mighty.* New York: Blue Sky Press.

Sleeter, C. E., & Grant, C. A. (1998). *Making choices for multicultural education: Five approaches to race, class, and gender.* New York: MacMillan.

Soto, G. (1991). *Taking sides.* San Diego, CA: Harcourt Brace Jovanovich.

Speare, E. G. (1983). *The sign of the beaver.* Boston: Houghton Mifflin.

Storti, C. (1994). *Cross-cultural dialogues: 74 brief encounters with cultural difference.* Yarmouth, ME: Intercultural Press.

Taylor, M. D. (1976). *Roll of thunder, hear my cry.* New York: Dial Press.

Taylor, M. D. (1981). *Let the circle be unbroken.* New York: Dial Press.

Taylor, M. D., & Ginsburg, M. (1990). *Mississippi bridge.* New York: Dial Books for Young Readers.

Taylor, M. D., & Pinkney, J. (1975). *Song of the trees.* New York: Dial Press.

Thomas, J. R. & Howell, T. (1981). *The comeback dog.* New York: Houghton Mifflin/Clarion Books.

Walvoord, B., & Anderson, V. (1998). *Effective grading: A tool for learning and assessment.* San Francisco: Jossey-Bass.

Yolen, J. (1985). *The Holocaust: The devil's arithmetic.* Logan, IA: Perfection Learning.

Ethical Sensitivity Appendix

About the Authors

Darcia Narvaez, Ph.D., is Associate Professor of Psychology at the University of Notre Dame. She developed the Integrative Ethical Education model (initiated under the federally-funded Minnesota Community Voices and Character Education Project which she reported on at a Whitehouse conference). Previously at the University of Minnesota, she was executive director of the Center for the Study of Ethical Development and was director of the Center for Ethical Education at the University of Notre Dame. She is on the editorial boards of the *Journal of Educational Psychology* and the *Journal of Moral Education*. She has published in the *Journal of Educational Psychology, Developmental Psychology*, and has two award-winning books, *Postconventional Moral Thinking* (1999; with Rest, Bebeau & Thoma) and *Moral Development, Self and Identity* (2004; with Lapsley).

Leilani Gjellstad Endicott, Ph.D., is Director of Research Integrity and Compliance at Walden University. She received her Ph.D. in child psychology at the University of Minnesota. Her areas of research include developmental psychopathology, post-traumatic stress, program evaluation, moral cognition, intercultural development, and creative arts therapy. Some of her research and community intervention partners include Army Community Services, Tubman Family Alliance, Little Earth United Tribes, the University of Minnesota Child and Adolescent Psychiatry Department and the Minnesota Department of Education. She has taught philosophy of science, research ethics, developmental psychology, social psychology, research methods, advanced research methods, introductory psychology, and psychological theories for the helping professions at the University of Minnesota, St. Olaf College, and Walden University.